G000152585

JACKLIN

JACKLIN

The Champion's Own Story

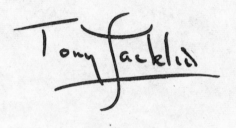

HODDER AND STOUGHTON
LONDON SYDNEY AUCKLAND TORONTO

FOREWORD

When Tony Jacklin won the Greater Jacksonville Open in 1968, and became the first British player since Henry Cotton to win a top tournament on the U.S. circuit, I immediately cabled the P.G.A. offices in London, expressing my absolute delight at his victory.

Not only had I been his playing partner in the last two rounds, and therefore as near to his triumph as anyone, but I also saw the realisation of a great personal ambition of my own. Golf is the greatest international game, and I've had the happiest experience of playing in almost every country of the world. But none more so than at the first home of golf, in Great Britain, whether at St. Andrews, or Birkdale, or Troon or at any other great championship course. And it always seemed a miscarriage of justice that no British player had for so many years proved himself to be a real champion at the highest international level.

Tony has put the matter aright, and I salute him, and his victories at Jacksonville, at Lytham, and then this year at Chaska.

I first played with him in the World Cup in Tokyo in the fall of 1966. I knew immediately that, though seemingly overawed by the occasion (and, perhaps by his playing partners!), here was a young player of enormous potential. And by the time I partnered him again the following year, at the U.S. Masters at Augusta, I felt sure Tony could be a champion.

He has many attributes on and off the course. Now he is a confident and aggressive player, but he had already found way back in 1967 a secret that escapes so many foreign players who come to the U.S.A. in their search for golfing success. This is the ability to adapt, to play on unfamiliar courses, to mix with new people, to travel vast distances week after week, and yet to feel at home. This, above all, has been one of the keys to his meteoric success.

Tony is now twenty-six. He has already won the American and British Open Championships. I was twenty-seven when I won my first Open, and I envy him his future, wishing him, and this book, every success.

Arnold Palmer

CONTENTS

ILLUSTRATIONS

Acknowledgements

All the photographs throughout the book are by Frank Gardner or Chris Smith, and are acknowledged by their respective initials. The front cover photograph, by Frank Gardner, is of Tony Jacklin at the U.S. Open at Chaska. The back cover, by Chris Smith, shows Jacklin returning to the clubhouse after rain had suspended play on the first day of the 1970 British Open at St. Andrews.

'I wish to acknowledge the significant part played by Jack Wood in the writing of this book. His help and advice made it entirely possible.'

I

The United States Open Championship
Chaska, Minnesota, 1970

I

The United States Open Championship
Chaska, Minnesota, 1970

Vivien and I checked in at the Thunderbird Motel on the outskirts of Minneapolis three days before the U.S. Open and I was not surprised when I opened a golf magazine to find myself rated twentieth behind Masters winner Billy Casper among the contenders for the championship. Play began on election day in Britain and the third week in June was to end with the shock win of Mr Edward Heath and the even bigger surprise of my seven stroke victory at Chaska.

My form in the previous weeks had not been exactly inspiring. In the Tournament of Champions at Rancho la Costa I had finished joint second with Gary Player and Casper behind runaway winner Frank Beard but at Atlanta, Memphis, Kemper and the Western Open you had to look in the small type way behind the winners to find the name Jacklin. In fact I missed the cut at Memphis and the general build-up of my game was not as I would have liked before a bid for a title last won by a Briton fifty years earlier.

But tournament golf is a game of very fine shades. I kept telling myself that as holder of the British Open I must have some sort of chance if only I could rediscover the putting touch which had deserted me. There had been nothing wrong with my striking of the ball from tee to green for a couple of weeks but I just had not been able to hole the ten-foot putts, the ones that are so essential in the big golf game as we know it today.

Chaska was half an hour's drive from the motel and when we arrived at the Hazeltine National club there were already rumblings that the newly created course was not exactly a hit with many of the leading players. Dave Hill, who was to finish second, incurred the wrath of officials later in the week by suggesting that the whole place should be ploughed up. 'All it needs,' said the edgy, ever controversial Dave, 'is eighty acres of corn and some cows.' The locals took exception to this and when I played with Hill in the third round a number of people in the crowd mooed as he walked along the fairways.

I have been asked many times if this upset me or affected my concentration. The answer is negative for on that day I followed my opening rounds of seventy-one and seventy with another seventy and increased my lead to four strokes. If there is one thing the travelling and intense competition of recent years has taught me it is to put everything from my mind but the shot I am about to play. The game presents enough problems without getting mixed up in what is happening to the other fellows. Dave was, in fact, quite a pleasant chap to play with— we discussed our shots and never at any time did he seem to be affected by the reaction of the crowd to his outburst about the course.

On the second practice day I had really got the feel of the course with its seemingly endless run of dog leg holes and blind shots; but I was still not holing those putts. Then came a meeting on the practice putting green with Jim Yancey, the brother of

Bert, who has been one of my closest friends since I first went to play regularly in the U.S. at the beginning of 1968.

Jim watched me putt and suggested that having lined up the putt and set the blade behind the ball I should switch my eyes to the hole and strike the ball with my eyes still on the hole. He said that nothing would be gained by looking at the ball and since I had the mechanics of the stroke embedded in my consciousness it would be simple to strike it while still looking at the target.

The putts began to drop from all over the place and I could feel the confidence rushing into me. I played another nine holes practice that afternoon and although on the course I did not hold the hole in my eyes as I struck the ball I took a much longer look at the hole before making the stroke. In this way I had a complete mental picture of where I wanted the ball to go and if any one thing helped me to win it was that chance meeting with Jim Yancey.

Casper was, as I say, favourite and immediately behind him the pollsters placed 1968 winner Lee Trevino and Player who had won in 1965. The latter pair were first and second in the season's money list and both had demonstrated regularly their ability to rise to the big occasion. That night I looked at the Open Form Chart in Golf Digest again and said to Viv that if my new putting confidence stayed with me I might have a chance in an event for which I had tied for twenty-sixth place in my only previous attempt the year before.

Viv was having her own problems. Bradley, now seven months, was about to cut his first tooth and he had also discovered that he could stand up in his cot and almost shake the thing to pieces. He seemed to find the middle of the night the ideal time to do this and we tried to get another room so that he and his mother could cope with his tooth cutting and cot shaking on their own and leave me to get some sleep. But the motel was full and poor Viv cat winked her way through most nights so that she could grab Bradley whenever he woke.

I was drawn to play with Casper and Steve Melnyk, the U.S. amateur champion, in the first two rounds and when we got to the course rain and a strong wind of something like forty miles an hour increased my feeling of confidence. It is untrue to say that American players cannot cope with rough conditions but I had been brought up in them and played much of my golf in them. In spite of this I would have questioned the sanity of anyone who told me, before we teed off on that first blustery morning, that I was about to set off on a great adventure in which I would shoot sub-par rounds of 71-70-70-70 and open up so much daylight between myself and my nearest rival. Win, maybe, because I always believe that when everything clicks I have the game and the temperament to do that but lead all the way and win by such a margin. Ridiculous.

The 'cowpatch' took heavy toll of many big names that first day. Arnold Palmer took seventy-nine, Gary Player eighty and Jack Nicklaus eighty-one. Jack said after his nine over par morale shaker that someone might still win with one round in the eighty region and Larry Ziegler, one of the longest hitters and most colourful youngsters on the tour, forecast that 300 for the four rounds would be good enough to land the £12,500 prize.

With almost half the field taking eighty and more the scoreboard took on a farcical look and the locker rooms echoed with tales of disaster. Dan Jenkins was to write in *Sports Illustrated* the following week, 'The touring pros have been making it increasingly plain in recent years that they object to any track with a tree, a pond or a par five that can't be reached with a drive and a swizzle stick.' He added that many of the big names played over the 'farm' as if they had hoes in their hands, but my concern throughout four days during which the cramp got worse and the tension almost unbearable was my own game and not that of the others.

This is what competitive golf is all about in my view. You do your best, keep your head, isolate yourself from everything around you. The fact that someone else is shooting a double bogey can in no way affect the swing you yourself make at the ball.

Billy Casper is without question one of the easiest men in the world to play with. He always knows exactly what he wants to do and there can seldom have been a top class player who takes so little time over his shots. He is a complete professional and there have been times through the years when I have envied him his ability to go straight to the ball and play it. His last shot in the Masters of 1970 from a trap right of the green illustrated this. . . . straight into the sand and a gentle splash out near the pin.

As I have said, the wind was strong and the conditions very much to my liking. I said after the first round that I would be happy if the wind blew all week. The terrain was lightly hilly, there was the odd bald spot, but after round one we had a perfectly calm day, a cold and overcast one for the third round and then on that Sunday of so much joy ideal conditions again. How else could I feel looking back on that climax which took me from a four stroke lead to victory by a margin which some thought was a record but which on investigation turned out to be two less than Jim Barnes had enjoyed back in 1921. The statisticians found that Ralph Guldhal had won by six shots in 1938 at Cherry Hills and this had been matched by Ben Hogan when he came home almost alone at Oakmont in 1953. So the margin was the second biggest.

I began the first round with a birdie three and as things turned out this was the way I finished at the seventy-second hole. Between these two birdies so many things happened, so much tension built up, so many scores by the great stars soared, and through it all I found myself in the role of pacemaker and an unexpected pacemaker at that. Of course it was tough but I have always said that I prefer to lead because it means that behind you the other fellows have to make the birdie and eagle putts to catch you. It had happened at Royal Lytham the previous year when I began with a two stroke lead in the final round of the British Open and I was quite happy that it should happen again.

Jim Yancey's putting teach-in had given me the confidence I needed when I took my putter for the first time in this championship which was to change my status from that of a home bred winner of the British Open to one who could win a championship abroad, and there was more than a little glow as my putt from fifteen feet broke in from the right and settled into the hole. The sort of start which does wonders for the guy who makes it.

Vivien was in the crowd—it would take more than a little teething trouble and cot-rocking from Bradley to keep her away from any tournament in which I play ... and I sensed that something good might be going to happen to the whole Jacklin family. But golf has a habit of slapping you down when you feel like this and after a duck hook from the tee and a topped two iron followed by a minor flirtation with the trees with my seven iron third I had to settle for a bogey five.

I was again in trouble when a sand wedge caught the limb of a tree at the par five third. The ball plummeted down into a bunker but I managed to get out to two feet to save my par at this giant 585 hole. The downhill fourth hole is similar to the short sixteenth at Stoke Poges but longer and I got it going again with a five iron to within eighteen inches of the hole. For a long time it looked as if the ball might go in for an ace but in the exalted golfing company I was keeping I was happy to have a two. One under par again.

The fifth hole at Hazeltine presents a number of problems. In this first round I attacked it with a driver but after going into the deepish rough over the hill and on the left of the fairway I decided that from then on I would use a two iron from the tee. The hole has a dog leg right and from the rough I choked down on a somewhat lucky seven iron and the ball finished only two feet away. The start looked good (3-5-5-2-3) and looked even better after the sixth where I holed from thirty feet for a birdie three.

I made a mistake at the next when I misjudged just how hard the sand was after a three iron into a trap on the right. This is one of the poorer holes at Hazeltine for you have no chance of cutting the corner, and the water hazard just short of the green seldom comes into play for the second shot. Few people attempted to get up in two here and from the sand into which I played my third shot I went eighteen feet past and two putts brought me my first six.

The short holes gave me a wonderful boost in this first round for at the eighth 185 yards I hit a three wood into the near gale and holed a twenty-footer for my second two. After a par four at the ninth I took a chance with the wind behind me at the tenth, carried the trees, but hit a pitching wedge short and had to hole from seven feet for my par four.

I holed from thirty feet for a birdie at the twelfth. My second was unlucky after carrying one trap but going into another off the hard green, but for a long time I had been perfectly happy with my sand wedge and the shot from the sand went straight for the hole and in. Things were now looking good—it is amazing how in the last year or so I seem to have found a way of getting the ball out from bunkers near the hole. And this time I went one better.

The round continued to go well. After a regulation three at the short thirteenth after a five iron to the green, I parred the next two, both times bunkering my second shots, coming out to seven feet and holing the putts. With all those high scores in I began thinking that I might make a four under par 68 which would be good enough to send me into the second round with a handsome lead.

Then for a while the wheels came off. A two iron at the short sixteenth finished at the back left hand corner of the green and I three stabbed it, missing the second one from only three feet. Worse was to come at the next where I hit some trees and the ball dropped into the water to the right and short of the green.

This meant a penalty of one shot, and I ended the hole with a double bogey six. A par on the last gave me a seventy-one and a two shot lead over Bob Charles. It was a little early to think that way, but on the way back to the motel Viv and I wondered out loud whether as at Lytham eleven months earlier I might find myself fighting out the finish of another Open with Charles.

In the round I hit eight fairways, had six birdies, three bogeys and one double bogey, but had only twenty-seven putts. This was in complete contrast to my recent experience on the greens and if I could have found Jim Yancey when I got in I would have bought him the biggest scotch he had ever seen.

I said at the press interviews afterwards that the wind could keep blowing as hard as it liked as far as I was concerned but the weather was quieter the next day. Back at the Thunderbird we had a quiet meal, watched television for a while, then an early night, with Viv making sure that any noise from junior did not last long enough to disturb the old man.

Again Casper and Melnyk were my partners and after opening with two pars, the second of which followed another good recovery from sand, I had one of the worst holes of the championship. After a drive into the rough I duffed the second into sand, came out and into more sand and eventually holed from fifteen feet for a six.

Another long putt, this time from fourteen feet, dropped at the next after a three iron from the tee hit sand. I have always found the American crowds most generous and the cheer which went up when this second long putt dropped might have been for Casper or any of the American stars. I felt almost as much at home as I had done at Lytham the year before, and the cheers were good for me because I seem to respond to this sort of thing just as I used to get upset early in my career with British crowds who appeared to defy you to do anything which would make them show their feelings. I am not talking of big events like our Open but in some of the smaller tournaments it was like playing in church.

I had been in sand three times in four holes and the routine did not change at the fifth which cost me a bogey five after a seven iron second into a bunker. Pars followed at the next two with the 563 yard seventh well out of range in two shots. I hit a good drive and four wood but still needed a six iron for my third.

At the ninth I tried to cut the corner but just failed to make it. Then I hit a good iron from the left rough and holed from eight feet for a welcome birdie to bring me back to one over for the round and level for the tournament. This was the start of a hot run which was to set me up for the rest of the championship.

A nine iron finished four feet away at the tenth and after a drive and three wood at the 590 yard eleventh I knocked a wedge to seven feet and holed the putt for my third birdie in a row. Pars followed at the next five but I was again in trouble at the seventeenth where I had crashed to a double bogey on the first day.

This time I pulled a two iron from the tee under the trees. Although only 344 yards long it is impossible to go for the green because of trees on either side of the fairway and the two lakes which guard the approach to the pin. Two choices were open to me, one to be cautious and play out sideways, the second to go for the green with a low shot under the branches and between the lakes.

I decided to have a go and this was perhaps the most vital shot of the 281 I played. Having taken that caning here in round one I decided to try and get even with the hole and few shots have made me feel happier than the punched five iron which stayed low under the trees and sailed on to within four feet of the flag. The putt went in and what had looked a certain bogey, maybe worse, became a birdie and I was two under for the day.

There was some suggestion that a lady marker had trodden on my ball after a three iron into deep grass at the last but I played the ball from where it lay and holed from twelve feet for my par and a seventy. This time I hit nine fairways, had twenty-nine putts, four birdies and two bogies. The Americans are hot on statistics and within a few minutes of finishing I was told that nineteen of the sixty-six U.S. Opens played had been won by the leader at the half way stage. The course had been very different this second day and I said at the time that it had been like playing Hazeltine in two different seasons.

The third day began with an announcement that Hill, my new partner, had been fined one hundred and fifty dollars for his comments on the course. Dave is an outspoken character and suggested when he paid the fine that he write out a cheque for another one hundred and fifty dollars, so that he could have another go. It was, oddly enough, the birthday of Robert Trent Jones, the man who designed the course.

Hill is a beautiful swinger of a golf club and plays the sort of golf I enjoy watching. Many thought that playing with the man who was at the centre of so much controversy would put the pressure on me, but, as I say, I have learned to live with these things and pay attention not to what the other fellow is doing or saying but to what is happening to me.

The day was not as bright but it was good for golf. I began with two pars with Hill dropping a shot at the first and birdied the third with an eight foot putt from right of the hole after a drive, two iron and wedge. This good start was what I needed after entering the second half of the Open with a two shot lead; but I bogied the fifth, three putting from no more than six yards.

My second to the sixth, a seven iron finished at the back of the green but I chipped down to a foot to save the par. I was bunkered at the next but getting some distance from the sand with a four iron, I made the front edge with an eight iron, and got down in two more. The crowds were having their fun with Hill but for me the tension suddenly began to tell—my legs felt heavy and I was hit with a sort of cramp. I have known this sort of thing before and refused to let it worry me when I got down to making my shots. But it was a critical moment for me just a round and a half away from achieving the second great ambition of a golfing lifetime.

I came out of the left rough and holed from nine feet for a birdie three at the ninth, parred the tenth, and birdied the eleventh when I wedged to twelve feet and holed the putt after a drive and three wood along the centre of the fairway. I almost made the water from the sand with my second to the twelfth but managed to get a wedge up high to within four feet of the hole for my par.

After four more regulation pars, I was back at the seventeenth, that troublesome hole so heavily criticised by many of the players, and again I was in a spot. My tee shot, a two iron finished behind the trees and at first I thought of laying up short of the green. But Hill was bang in the middle of the fairway and in a position to make three so I attacked again and hit an eight iron high over the trees eight yards from the hole. I keep thinking of shots which swung things my way, for there were probably half a dozen of them over the four rounds. This was certainly one of them, and the gamble almost paid extra with a sensational birdie for I only just missed the putt. But in view of the certain bogey I would have made playing safe I was more than happy with the par.

The eighteenth brought me more trouble but I managed to chip close to the hole from rough left of the green and get my four. The 70 I happily signed for put me four shots ahead of Hill. I hit eight fairways, had 29 putts, one bogey at the fifth and three birdies at the third, ninth and eleventh.

I had seen the scoreboard after nine holes and knew that Gay Brewer was only two strokes back then, but although I like to know what is happening I just kept saying to myself that if I was to win it would be because I made the good shots and kept my score going. My four stroke lead was the highest after fifty-four holes on the tour all season and I knew that if I could keep the tempo going and the swing slow I had a great chance of going home in a couple of days' time as holder of both Open titles.

The cramp was bad. I am sure it had a lot to do with the mounting tension and when we got back to the Thunderbird I got some rubbing cream and gave my legs a good massage. Viv wanted to do it for me but she is strong, this wife of mine, and in the past when she has given me a massage it has hurt like hell. So I told her to look after Bradley and did my own massage.

We talked a lot over dinner about home and of the hectic schedule of TV matches I would be playing in Britain before defending my British Open title. Both of us knew just what victory would mean in terms of cash and our future but tried to steer clear of the subject. Viv is a wonderful help at times like this and if I start day dreaming, and the temptation was great that night at the Thunderbird, she brings me back to earth with some little reminder of the tough times we have had and will probably have again.

I slept fairly well after taking a few calls. It is amazing the number of people who want to reassure you that 'everything's going to be fine, Tony', and when I got to the club next morning for my usual half hour practice session there were dozens of telegrams and cables from friends all over the world. If I ever had any friends in the post office at Scunthorpe I doubt if I have them now.

I was worried all morning as I played with Bradley that the cramp would come back on the course, so sat for a while on the edge of a pool full of spa water at the motel. I did not want to go right in as I have found that swimming or taking a bath just before playing relaxes the muscles too much.

When I got to my locker I saw a notice with the one word 'tempo' pinned to the door. Tom Weiskopf, another great friend from the U.S. tour, knows almost as much about my game as I do and thought it as well to remind me that in this the final test I must swing slow. This was one of a number of kind gestures towards me by friends and people I had never met; but I could have done without the hours grilling by press, radio and TV before I set off on the last round with Brewer. I was, of course delighted to be playing with Gay who is one of the finest and most gentle people of them all. If I could not play perhaps the most vital round of my career with him then I could play it with no one.

My manager, Mark McCormack, called me at the motel and

after a while asked me what colour slacks and roll neck I would be wearing. He could not disguise the fact that he was more than a little jumpy, and after a while suggested that I go for the lavender top I had worn when winning the British Open. I agreed that this might be lucky but as I played with Bradley I got to thinking what the heck was I doing wondering about lucky colours and that sort of thing when four shots clear with a round to go.

I gave up superstitions of this sort a while ago. My mother always told Lynn, my sister, and me that green was unlucky and we were never allowed to wear anything with green on if we were going in for an examination at school or doing anything else special. Once, playing in Ireland, I thought back to those days when I had three sixty-eights in a tournament at Clandeboyes—and an eighty-three in the other round when I was wearing green. Maybe mum had something after all.

At Jacksonville in 1968 I decided that I must get rid of this colour thing, and deliberately chose green before going out for my last round and first victory in the U.S. Now, in Minneapolis, I went against Mark's suggestion and chose lime green slacks with a black pullover. It was some sort of reverse thinking. I just did not want to feel that anything but my own golf game could possibly have anything to do with the shots I made. I have drilled myself to think positively whatever the situation, however tough the going, and considered the wearing of a particular colour against this thinking. But maybe Mark was to be right—he had his lavender in the last match after all when Brewer appeared wearing a sweater of that colour.

The atmosphere was charged in the way it had been at Lytham such a short time ago. But this time no family around, no car loads of friends from Scunthorpe, few immediately recognisable faces. Somehow Viv and I were there in the vast acres of Minnesota alone as the crowds flocked through the gates to see the 'Little limey kid Jacklin' defend his lead against Hill, Brewer, Boros and the rest of them. It is odd that people refer to me often as both 'little' and a 'kid'. I am a little over 5ft. 10in. with shoes, and weigh 12st. 2lb. People find this astonishing but I can assure them the figures are accurate. And no doubt there are times when I look younger than twenty-six, but I could not possibly have done at Chaska. I felt when it was all over that I had put on at least twenty years in four days when I found as the pressure rose my appetite grew less and my temper shorter and shorter. But Vivien understood, and without her and Bradley around at such times I truly do not know how I would cope.

This was the position when Gay and I knocked in the final practise putts and went to the first tee. Jacklin, five under; Hill, one under; Brewer, one over; Boros, two over; Bob Lunn, three over; Gene Littler and Ken Still four over; Randy Wolff, Richard Crawford and Bruce Devlin, five over.

Hill, who had been in the first ten six times during the season and, with earnings of 67,581 dollars, was about 11,000 dollars up on me, looked to be the danger man. But, he was playing immediately in front of Gay and me so that I would know how he was doing. I could therefore adjust my tactics as the situation demanded, play conservatively if all I had to do was hold on to the lead, be bolder should Dave start some sort of charge. It was an extremely comfortable situation to find myself in and it was probably an indication of how I felt that the leg cramp which had been so bad during the desperate pressure of the third round hardly affected me in this final run to the post. Although Hill has a reputation for coming from behind, I felt as confident as anyone can feel in a game like golf where one bad shot can change the position so dramatically. I knew, because it is part of sporting folklore that Casper had pulled back seven shots from Palmer in the 1965 Open, but having played three sub par rounds there was surely nothing to stop me breaking par again in the best golfing conditions we had enjoyed all week. That is the way my reasoning went, that if I could shoot seventy-one Hill would have to make a sixty-six to beat me and Brewer, surely the only other danger, a sixty-four. Somehow scores like that were not on.

I made the first two greens with a drive and eight iron and two putted them both for pars. The third was again unreachable in two but I got home with a safe five after a drive, two iron and wedge but then missed a good birdie chance on the short fourth where my five iron finished only five feet away. The birdie I was looking for came at the fifth where I holed from seven feet after a two iron from the tee and a five iron just left of the stick. I heard at this time that Dave was going steadily but was not making any real charge and with this birdie under my belt after pretty solid pars for openers I felt real good.

I missed another good chance at the next where a putt from only four and a half feet never looked like going in and then wham!. Trouble. Two bogeys and it felt like I had been kicked in the stomach. Viv was somewhere around and it would have been nice to have a word with her. It is difficult to describe how I felt, one minute everything going for me, the next that odd feeling of loneliness, isolation which is heightened by the fact that there seems to be millions of people around. But none of them can help. No one could help because when I finally took up my hitting position the whole thing was within the limits of the eternal and sometimes infernal triangle—a golf club, a golf ball and me.

At the seventh my drive hit a tree on the right and my second with a four wood finished on a bare lie. I had hit my first bad shot of the afternoon and was paying for it. I tried to get distance from that patchy bit of ground but finished in the crowd and needed a fourth shot with a short iron to get the green. I am told this is what happened and that I two putted for six. Certainly I had a six to drop back to level par but even now what happened is wrapped up in some sort of memory fog. I wanted to win so much, and to win by as many shots as I could, and here with just twelve holes to play I felt that I might be going into some sort of skid which would wreck everything when it seemed almost impossible for a crash like this to come.

The short eighth, with water in front of the green, was one of the most heavily criticised and Hill had bogeyed it in the second and third rounds. It had been good to me all week. I hit the green with a three wood against the wind in the first round and holed from twenty feet for a two. After a three there in round two, I had only just missed a two on the third day. Now the news came back that Hill had just made three but after a satisfactory tee shot I three putted for only the third time in the tournament. I could not have chosen a worse time.

With Hill out in a level par thirty-six my lead had been cut to three. The next few minutes were perhaps the most critical I had known. More trouble here and I would be only two in front. As someone wrote of that time, 'For a moment what had looked like a massacre threatened to turn into a golf tournament again.' I set my tee shot off on what I thought a good line but the ball finished in the rough. There is some strange chemistry between golf crowds and players which is at its most potent at times like these, and I could feel that many among the thousands watching this climax to an astonishing week wanted me to pull out of the spin almost as much as I wanted to myself. The happy chatter of a gallery watching someone making birdies seems to be stilled when the wheels look as if they are coming off the victory wagon and I sensed that an awful lot of American hearts were beating just a little faster for me when I went into the rough.

The lie was a reasonable one and I was able to hit the green with a four iron. The depression lifted a little and then blew off across the cattle and wheat plains of Minnesota when I holed tht putt from thirty feet for a birdie three. This was without doubt the most vital putt of the week and luck was with me. I hit it a little strong and, as it raced for the hole, I had the horrible mental picture of the ball missing and finishing four or five feet past. But it hit the back of the hole, bounced fully a foot in the air and then bolted down out of sight again like a rabbit going underground in the face of danger. I have had a few spells at home since Chaska and often find myself thinking back to those three holes when it seemed so likely that I would blow my lead, or much of it. And of that putt charging across the green, slamming against the back of the hole, up and down again, and in.

From that moment life seemed good again and in spite of what there was for me at the end of this particular golfing rainbow I actually enjoyed playing the last nine holes. And the nearer I got to the end of this marvellous four-day battle the more I enjoyed it.

The tenth dog legs to the left, and after a perfectly placed drive I hit a wedge ten feet right of the hole and knocked in the putt. I was one under for the day after successive birdies, and the clamming agony of a couple of holes back almost forgotten as the crowd shouted encouragement and roared, 'Go to it, Tony baby!' We were all involved now and it is so much better to be involved in a victory march than the wake which for a while seemed likely.

I must now be content to defend a lead which seemed impregnable. Conservative golf has never been a feature of my game and through the years I have been told that I take too many gambles, but with a second Open championship in eleven months only eight holes away I decided to settle for pars and welcome any birdie that came along.

The eleventh, a dog leg right, was unreachable in two so I hit a drive wide and left of the trees, a three wood, wedge short of the hole and two putts gave me my par. I was six under par and knew that if I could keep these pars going nothing could stop me.

I made the twelfth green with a three wood and five iron and almost holed the putt from thirty feet. A three at the thirteenth after a five iron left of the pin took me into the final five holes, the stretch of which Hazeltine designer, Robert Trent Jones, wrote before play began, 'It is over these finishing five that the tournament will be won and lost.'

The fourteenth is not a dog leg in the sense that eight of the holes at Hazeltine are, but it turns just slightly right and from the tee one can see nothing but woods. A two iron finished about 140 yards from the green and I played my eight iron purposely well left of the pin to wipe out any chance of making the sand trap on the right of the green. An overhit shot here can fall away into thick rough and woods but I was safely on and down in two putts.

I placed a good drive right of the bunker on the left of the fifteenth fairway, hit another good wood between more bunkers along the fairway, then a wedge to the small green with its four menacing bunkers. The news that Hill was making no impression kept filtering back and when that wedge finished only eight feet from the hole I felt for the first time it was impossible for me to lose. At Lytham, the previous year, I had not known that final realisation that I was about to become champion until I had hit my second shot to the eighteenth green. This time I had three holes to enjoy the experience. My legs felt a little tired but although Viv said afterwards that she had never seen me looking so drawn and strained I felt pretty good.

Two putts kept me one under for the day and so to the long par three sixteenth. The green there has a bracelet of three traps running from left centre of the green back down to the right-hand edge and a pushed tee shot could bounce off the right-hand slope into Lake Hazeltine. My two iron finished safely on the front edge and although a little strong with the first putt I made the return for a par.

At last I played the seventeenth well. The fairway slopes left to right, and I hit a four iron into the safe spot and a wedge to the front edge. With so much danger around this was no time for heroics although I could now afford the luxury of a trip into one of the two ponds. I played the hole exactly the way I wanted to and with two putts stayed six under.

I have been asked hundreds of times since that afternoon of June the twenty-first how it felt to stand on the eighteenth tee with such a huge lead. I knew that the B.B.C. were transmitting the A.B.C. pictures by satellite and thought of home and the family and friends who would be watching, and of the celebrations in the bars of Potters Bar and Scunthorpe Golf Clubs.

I drove over the bunker on the left side of the fairway and a four iron took me thirty feet from the pin. The reception was fantastic, and as I walked into that huge horseshoe of people I knew I could now take six putts and still win. But winning was no longer enough . . . I wanted to win by as many as possible, stay under par in each of the four rounds, make this final moment as memorable as I could for Viv and all those on both sides of the Atlantic who had done so much to make it possible.

At Royal Lytham I had left my first putt half an inch short of the hole. Now I was determined to be strong enough and from the moment I hit it I knew the putt was in. The long, often adventurous journey was over. A Briton had won for the first time since Ted Ray in 1920 and only Jim Barnes in 1921 had won by a bigger margin.

I like a drink, the occasional cigarette, and enjoyed a few of both in the next few hours. The people who run Lord Fletchers, an English style eating place in Minneapolis, had already delivered a crate of beer to the clubhouse and after the joy of those last few holes and the mists of the presentation ceremony we set about celebrating.

Dave Hill refused to come out for the presentation. The day before, Hill had been asked if he would play in the British Open. 'If they ever found me over there again,' he said, 'they'd know I died and somebody shipped my body to the wrong place.' But I am sure his refusal to line up with me at the prize-giving had nothing to do with me personally. Dave is wound like a spring and his reaction was that of a bitterly disappointed man who with others considers Hazeltine and its dog leg holes and bare patches an unsuitable site for a great championship.

We drove back to the Thunderbird where I telephoned home. They were of course all thrilled but my mother seemed almost as excited at the news that Bradley had cut his first tooth. After that call we took the room telephone off and went out for a quiet meal with Ken Gordon, a member of the Royal and Ancient, and some friends.

The next day I would have liked to have slept into the afternoon but there were interviews and calls from Mark McCormack and lots of other people. I kept thinking back to the vital moments—of those times of crisis at the seventeenth and of the birdies at the ninth and tenth in the last round.

CHASKA

ROUND BY ROUND ANALYSIS

ROUND ONE

Hole

1. Drive, wedge, fifteen foot putt. Birdie 3.
2. Hooked drive, topped two iron, seven iron, two putts. Bogie 5.
3. Drive, two iron, sand wedge, sand wedge to two feet, one putt. Par 5.
4. Five iron to eighteen inches, one putt. Birdie 2.
5. Drive into left rough, choked down seven iron to two feet, one putt. Birdie 3.
6. Drive, seven iron, thirty foot putt. Birdie 3.
7. Drive, three iron into right trap, sand wedge, wedge, two putts. Bogie 6.

8. Three wood, twenty foot putt. Birdie 2.
9. Drive, two iron, two putts. Par 4.
10. Drive, pitching wedge short, two putts. Par 4.
11. Drive, three wood, eight iron, two putts. Par 5.
12. Drive, six iron into trap, holed from sand from thirty feet. Birdie 3.
13. Five iron, thirty feet right, two putts. Par 3.
14. Two iron, seven iron into trap, sand wedge to seven feet, one putt. Par 4.
15. Drive, three wood, three iron into right trap, out to seven feet, one putt. Par 5.
16. Two iron, three putts. Bogie 4.
17. Fat four iron, six iron, hit trees and into water, eight iron, two putts. Double bogie 6.
18. Drive, four wood, two putts. Par 4.

Total 71

ROUND TWO
Hole
1. Drive, five iron, two putts. Par 4.
2. Drive, seven iron into sand, sand wedge, one putt. Par 4.
3. Drive into left rough, second into sand, sand wedge into another bunker, sand wedge, two putts. Bogie 6.
4. Three iron into trap, sand wedge to fourteen feet, one putt. Par 3.
5. Two iron, seven iron into trap, sand wedge, two putts. Bogie 5.
6. Three wood into trees, seven iron, two putts. Par 4.
7. Drive, four wood, six iron, two putts. Par 5.
8. Four iron, two putts. Par 3.

9. Drive into left rough, eight iron to eight feet, one putt. Birdie 3.
10. Three wood, nine iron to four feet, one putt. Birdie 3.
11. Drive, three wood, sand wedge to seven feet, one putt. Birdie 4.
12. Drive, six iron, two putts. Par 4.
13. Five iron, two putts from thirty feet. Par 3.
14. Two iron, wedge, two putts. Par 4.
15. Drive, four wood, nine iron, two putts. Par 5.
16. Two iron, two putts. Par 3.
17. Two iron into trees, five iron to four feet, one putt. Birdie 3.
18. Drive, three iron, wedge, one putt. Par 4.

Total 70

ROUND THREE

Hole
1. Drive, eight iron, two putts. Par 4.
2. Drive, three iron, two putts. Par 4.
3. Drive, two iron, wedge, one putt from eight feet. Birdie 4.
4. Five iron, two putts. Par 3.
5. Two iron, seven iron, three putts from eighteen feet. Bogie 5.
6. Drive, seven iron to back left of green, chip to eighteen inches, one putt. Par 4.
7. Drive into bunker, four iron, eight iron, two putts. Par 5.
8. Two iron, two putts from twenty feet. Par 3.
9. Drive into left rough, nine iron, holed putt from nine feet. Birdie 3.
10. Drive, five iron, two putts from forty feet. Par 4.
11. Drive, three wood, wedge, one putt from twelve feet. Birdie 4.

12. Drive into bunker, five iron, hit trees, wedge to one foot, one putt. Par 4.
13. Five iron, two putts. Par 3.
14. Two iron, seven iron through trees, two putts. Par 4.
15. Drive, three wood, wedge, two putts. Par 5.
16. Two iron two putts. Par 3.
17. Pulled two iron thirty yards behind trees, eight iron over trees to green, two putts. Par 4.
18. Drive, three wood into left rough, chip to three feet, one putt. Par 4.

Total 70

ROUND FOUR

Hole
1. Drive, eight iron to fifteen feet, two putts. Par 4.
2. Drive, eight iron, two putts from twenty feet. Par 4.
3. Drive, two iron, wedge, two putts. Par 5.
4. Five iron, two putts from five feet. Par 3.
5. Two iron, five iron to seven feet, one putt. Birdie 3.
6. Drive, four iron, two putts from four and a half feet. Par 4.
7. Drive into trees, four wood, three iron into crowd, eight iron, two putts. Bogie 6.
8. Five iron, three putts. Bogie 4.
9. Drive, four iron, one putt from thirty feet. Birdie 3.
10. Drive, wedge, one putt from ten feet. Birdie 3.
11. Drive, three wood, wedge, two putts from short of pin. Par 5.
12. Three wood, five iron, two putts from thirty feet. Par 4.
13. Five iron, two putts from thirty feet. Par 3.
14. Two iron, eight iron, two putts. Par 4.
15. Drive, four wood, wedge, two putts from eight feet. Par 5.

16. Two iron, two putts. Par 3.

17. Four iron, eight iron, two putts. Par 4.

18. Drive, five iron, one putt from thirty feet. Birdie 3.

Total 70

Putting analysis over four rounds.

Three three putts, one hundred and twenty putts in all.

II

The British Open Championship
St. Andrews, 1970

II

The British Open Championship
St. Andrews, 1970

Jack Nicklaus, the most formidable figure in modern golf and perhaps the finest striker in the history of the game, sat dejectedly in the R. & A. scorers' caravan just outside the grey walls of the game's headquarters. Thirty yards away his fellow American Doug Sanders was about to putt from three feet above the hole for golf's oldest and most valued title and a fortune in endorsement contracts.

Jack and I had handed in our cards and were watching the action on television. At least I was. Nicklaus sat there head in hands and said repeatedly, 'Every guy must win at St. Andrews if he is to be among the greats. I've blown it. There is no way Doug can miss that putt. Who wants to be second here? No one.'

Before Sanders set himself over the ball I tried to reason with Jack that the putt was far from the easy one it looked. I figured it this way; that Doug had not known such tension for a long time; that the putt was slightly downhill with a quite vicious break to the right; and that it had to be hit very firmly or it would slide right at the last moment.

I said to the big fellow who seemed so convinced that any moment now he would be second, 'I know we can't do it. But that's an awful putt for Doug to have at a time like this. He has got to give it a rap but will he because a miss at the speed he must hit it will give him a bad one back. I would give you £10,000 for your chance of winning.'

Jack made a not too successful effort to smile. I watched the putt do what it always threatened to do, break quickly near the hole and finish on the right. Nicklaus could not believe it as everyone in the caravan shouted, 'He's missed it.' It is history now that the next day he went out and after once holding a four stroke lead finally survived by the narrowest margin to win the 1970 Open.

The eighteenth again produced a dramatic finale to the play-off. Nicklaus, who had driven the green each time when second to the late Tony Lema in 1964, unpeeled the sweater which all week had been an essential part of our golfing garb and went for the big one. The ball sailed past the pin and settled in fluffy grass at the back of the green—a drive of 370 yards.

Sanders drove down the middle and pitched five feet short. No golfer all week, maybe no golfer ever, had been faced with a second shot on the eighteenth on the Old Course from the spot where Nicklaus found himself. The lie was downhill, and a trip down the nineteenth seemed almost as inevitable as victory had seemed for Sanders twenty-four hours before. Nicklaus pitched to eleven feet from a hanging lie. Then, after long preliminaries, he holed the putt. No one will ever know whether Doug would have holed his five footer, for the Nicklaus closer for a birdie three made such deliberation academic.

Although beaten after spending the afternoon on a tightrope with a heavy crash for a long time likely, Sanders must look back on the 1970 British Open as the championship in which he rediscovered himself as a golfer. His previous form had been bad enough to force him to play in the qualifying rounds, yet in spite of a second shot into the Swilken burn at the very first hole of the ninety he was to play, he went as near to winning as any man can. It is not quite true that he practises his swing in a telephone box, but he is said to be able to swing fully in the smallest room of his home in Texas.

Nicklaus, with whom I have fished and golfed a lot in the last few years, had won at Muirfield in 1966 and been second at Royal Birkdale and Carnoustie. I believe he values our title more highly than any other in golf and it is true to say that next to Arnold Palmer he has done more to bring the championship back to its old eminence than anyone.

He is content these days to concentrate on the big events and because of his habit of disappearing from the U.S. tour so regularly some have thought he would never regain his rightful position as the world's number one player. But those who had watched him in other previous months always felt that the trimmed down figure of this very great golfer would soon be in the winner's enclosure again.

His putting remains a problem, for his average at St. Andrews was thirty-four and half putts a round. Yet this was one per round better than on his only previous championship on the Old Course. But at the par five holes he is firing at the green from huge distances with long irons or woods and cannot be expected to be as accurate as lesser mortals who lay up in two and then pitch to the pin with a club designed for that purpose.

I was not too disappointed with my own attempt to defend the title, but at the same time I cannot remember ever feeling quite so sick about anything in my career as I did after dropping three shots in the last five holes when we resumed on the Thursday morning after being washed out the previous evening when eight under par and heading maybe for the course record. I am no prophet and golf is a game in which prophets usually come unstuck but I did feel that late afternoon after going out in twenty-nine and starting back with a birdie three that I might shoot a sixty-two or three. But who knows, and now, who cares.

The fact is that my final score for the first round was sixty-seven, two behind the leader Neil Coles, and my total at the end of it all was 286 (67-70-73-76). The opening sixty-seven put me level with Harold Henning, the Argentinian Molina, Maurice Bembridge and John Richardson, a Scot born in St. Andrews. We were all two behind Coles, one behind Tommy Horton, and a shot in front of a group which included Lee Trevino, Sanders, Nicklaus and Palmer. The start was good enough for me to remain Open champion had I played well enough later on.

Much was written and said about my hectic schedule before the Open began. I was, it is true, tremendously busy and I can say truly that I have never packed, or been forced to pack, as much into two weeks as I did at that time. But I am twenty-six, strong, quite fit without being able to run a mile in four minutes or anything like that, and in spite of the non-stop T.V. filming and playing and rushing around, I felt good when I got to the course from the beautiful house at Dundee where the Jacklin clan was installed in unforgettable splendour.

After reading some of the newspapers at breakfast I almost had another look in the mirror to make sure I was the same chap they were writing about. It was said that I was tired, too tense after the excitement of Chaska, and many seemed to think that I was in no shape to play in the Open. For a moment or two I thought it might be as well to send my father along to St. Andrews to defend the family honour. He plays off seven.

Although I had not played the course as often as I would have liked I had got to know it quite well with rounds there the previous Thursday and Friday and a third with Palmer on the Monday afternoon after we had done some filming in the morning. Then the day before the ball game got under way I rested at Glamis House with the family and friends, sleeping through until eleven in the morning and then playing darts and going for a walk.

Willie Hilton, my caddy who will, I hope, one day spend some time with me on the U.S. tour, went down to the somewhat limited practice area with me and I had my usual half hour's warm up. As I bashed away with various clubs, news travelled to us that Horton, who had gone out at the crack of dawn, was setting the pace with a sixty-six and that Sanders, who is more used to the dawn chorus on his way to bed than coming from it, had made sixty-eight. Before we began Coles had taken the lead with sixty-five, and I do not have to say that these figures were hardly comforting to someone just setting out in defence of his title.

I quickly appreciated why many of those early scores were so low. The Old Course with its par of seventy-two can never have played easier. The conditions were absolutely perfect. The slightest of breezes had sprung up after the early morning haar (Scottish for sea mist) and many of the holes which sometimes need two woods or a wood and long iron were reachable with a drive and wedge. It was pitch and putt stuff most of the time and I felt that with reasonable breaks I would not be far behind the leaders at the end of this first day.

Play had been delayed because of the haar and had it not been for this I would have been able to finish the round instead of being stranded midst the thunder and lightning and hail and rain which made for one of the unhappiest half hours I have ever spent on a golf course.

In spite of the easy conditions earlier I rate the run to the turn in twenty-nine as the best nine holes I have ever played. It was, I believe, the lowest score for either nine ever recorded at St. Andrews and twenty-nine matched the best outward half in an Open set at Royal Lytham by five times winner Peter Thomson and Tom Haliburton.

The first was a drive and a wedge and I holed from twelve feet for a three. At this hole later in the week the young American Tom Shaw was to have surely the most amazing five ever shot there. After a good drive Shaw put his second to the back of the green. The pin was at the front and with his putt much too strong the ball ran on into the burn. Tens of thousands have flirted with the burn and finished in it but few can have made it from the 'wrong' direction. Then Tom dropped out for four and holed his pitch to the delight of the huge crowds who were for this 110th Open bigger by thirty thousand than ever before. Eighty thousand people paid at the gate and someone estimated the total receipts from entrance money, T.V. fees and franchise payments to be in the region of £175,000. I think we can say that professional golf in Britain is back in the big time.

The second was again reachable with a drive and pitch and I holed from five feet for another three. Drive and wedge at the third, a fifteen foot putt for a third birdie. Someone in the crowd said rather loudly that this was ridiculous but I felt that I could

J.—4

keep it going and after a drive and five iron to the fourth I just shaved the hole and missed a fourth three.

With what breeze there was behind I made the 567 yard par five fifth with a drive and four wood and two putted for a birdie four. Two putts at the next for a par, a fourth three at the seventh with a six footer, a par three at the short eighth and then an enormous stroke of luck at the ninth where after a one iron from the tee I ran a pitching wedge straight into the hole for an eagle two. Come to think of it, sir, it was ridiculous . . . at least out there on the ninth.

This is the way I played those holes for the record twenty-nine.

First (374 yds.) Drive. Sand Wedge. 12 ft. putt.
Second (411 yds.) Drive. Pitching Wedge. 5 ft. putt.
Third (405 yds.) Drive. Pitching Wedge. 15 ft. putt.
Fourth (470 yds.) Drive. Five iron. Two putts.
Fifth (567 yds.) Drive. Four Wood. Two putts.
Sixth (414 yds.) Drive. Pitching Wedge. Two putts.
Seventh (364 yds.) Drive. Eight iron. 6 ft. putt.
Eighth (163 yds.) Six iron. Two putts.
Ninth (359 yds.) One iron. Pitching wedge into hole.
Figures:—3-3-3-4-4-4-3-3-2. Twenty-nine—Twelve putts.

Willie walked happily to the tenth tee and he said that he had never dreamed of such a celebration for the birth of his fifth child. She had been born the day before and he would call her Antonia or something to make him remember the day I shot twenty-nine at St. Andrews. I doubt if I will ever forget it either.

The tenth, fairly straightforward, was reached with a drive and wedge and the putt went in for another three. So if anybody does twenty-nine again for nine maybe they will take it easy on me and take four at the tenth. I often wonder why it is that at times like these one gets the feeling that the ball will go exactly where one wants whereas with what is the same swing and putting stroke things can be so different. Confidence builds up as the birdies come but the inspiration for this sort of scoring is something deeper. If it came in bottles the lucky fellow who made it would be onto his second million before he had counted the first.

I made pars at the next three which led someone to suggest that some old gentleman in the clubhouse had sent out instructions that the humbling of this long treasured strip of golfing territory along the Fifeshire coast must stop. Bad enough for a Scot to have done it but some young chap from Scunthorpe. . . .

The skies were blackening now and the first warning shots of thunder mumbled across the course. I had always believed that in the event of play being stopped all scores for the day were cancelled and I could not begin to tell you how I felt about that. The drive at fourteen went to the spot I had chosen and then as I settled down for a three wood to the green someone in the crowd shouted fore. I wondered who the devil would do such a thing, whether he was shouting at me. There was certainly no reason for this cry for we were a long way ahead of the pair behind and my partner Alex Caygill, with whom I travelled the British tour in the old days, was equally baffled.

My concentration, which had been pretty fierce so far, slipped for a moment and I pushed the three wood into the middle of a bush. I should, of course, have walked away from the ball when the shout of 'Fore' came but with the advance drops of a watershed patting into the turf I wanted to get on. By the time I got to the ball the monsoon was with us. Small lakes soon became big ones, the odd seagull appeared from nowhere and although we hung about under umbrellas for what seemed like several hours it was clear that it was curtains as far as any more golf was concerned.

Although good sense told me that I would have to drop out behind the bush when we resumed next morning I did not finally make up my mind. I marked the spot with a couple of tee pegs, gave the ball to Willie for safe keeping—it slept the night in a ball bag in the back of my car—and we were paddling in. The decision was taken that play would be resumed at seven-thirty the next morning and I rushed off to Dundee for a bath, dinner and as early a night as possible.

I felt sick that such a run had been interrupted but happy over the committee's decision. Maybe I would not get that sixty-four or less but what had gone before could not be a bad start in the defence of the title. Up at five-thirty, I had time for breakfast and a half-hour's warm-up, if that is the word, for this Thursday morning was wet and dreary and in complete contrast to the conditions in which I had begun the previous day.

With the rain belting down—if you have never been to Scotland I can assure you the rain in Spain has nothing on the stuff they get up there—I decided to drop behind the bush and with a penalty for picking out, was on the green in four. The first putt from quite some way almost went in but this was the nearest I came to holing anything decent in that dawn skirmish in the rain and on a sodden course.

My second to the fifteenth finished well left of the pin and, completely unable to judge the speed of the green, all I saw was the ball slowing up with a plume of spray behind it. The putt was seven feet or so and I was again short. Six-five . . . what the heck had happened to my sixty-four? I tried to tell myself that others, including Trevino, were suffering behind me and managed a par at the sixteenth. Both this one and the fifteenth must have presented birdie chances had conditions stayed the way they were for most of the previous day.

The seventeenth has claimed more victims than any hole at St. Andrews. The drive must carry the out of bounds land in front of the Old Course Hotel and after making the fairway I aimed to the right of the bunker which was guarding the flag. The shot was not quite strong enough and finished just short on the right hand side. The pitch, like those earlier putts, pulled up quickly and I missed for my third bogey of the morning. A drive, wedge and two putts on the eighteenth and I was wet and far from feeling warm towards whoever controls the weather as I signed for a sixty-seven.

By this time one or two brave spirits were already warding off the threat of pneumonia or worse with a taste of the hard stuff which at St. Andrews comes in bottles labelled R. & A. 1 and R. & A. 2 (I once asked the difference and was told threepence a nip!) but with another round due to begin in a couple of hours I settled for some coffee and dry clothes. As I walked down the stairs to the locker rooms after a short press conference I said loudly to no one in particular, 'What a son of a bitch!' And it was.

I cannot remember feeling less like playing than I did before the second round. I love golf and thoroughly enjoy the challenge of playing for major titles and prizes but now, after that shocking opening to the day, I had to try and shrug off all thought of what had gone before and do my best to get into the right frame of mind again. This mental thing is very big with me and Viv often says when we are travelling to a tournament that she senses I might do well. I have got to feel relaxed and yet have an edge to my game and I am only too aware that there are times when I play well below my best form. It is not that I do not try but sometimes there just seems no point in trying. It happens to us all . . . secretaries laddering their tights on the way to the office, housewives having 'one of those days', salesmen going through the familiar routine but knowing they haven't a chance of selling candy to a kid. But soon the starter would be calling Caygill and Jacklin to the tee and I told Willie that from that moment we would not mention the five holes I had played earlier. I had to think positively but seldom have I found it more difficult.

My second round began with five straight pars against one par and four birdies the day before but I then holed from thirty feet for a three at the sixth. I three putted the next on the huge plateau green at the beginning of the famed St. Andrews loop but kept it going fairly steadily with the course playing considerably harder and was satisfied after birdies at the thirteenth and sixteenth with a seventy. On the last green I just failed with a long putt to join Trevino (68-68) on 136 and felt much better about life after a couple of beers and dinner back at our 'castle'. Trevino was obviously going to be difficult to hold, for he was at the head of the U.S. money winners list for the season and his massive strength and low trajectory must prove formidable in the conditions.

Trevino had set his heart on victory. The thought of a Mexican from the tougher area of El Paso winning at St. Andrews appealed to him and he knew that the many products he endorses would have a much better chance of selling in Britain if he were crowned king on the Saturday evening. Maybe he wanted to win too badly. He was so much a master of the conditions and his game and there must have been some explanation for his bad start in the last round which sent him sliding back through the field after setting out with a two stroke lead.

Nicklaus was with me on 137, and two shots behind we had Coles, Henning, Sanders, John Richardson, the surprise packet of the championship, Horton and Clive Clark. This was the first tournament in which Richardson had played all season and although he faded at the finish he must have been delighted to wind up only nine shots behind Sanders and Nicklaus.

In the strong winds of the third day I felt that my timing was going and I could not get the feel of my putter, although I began with a birdie three from twelve yards after only just carrying the burn. Trevino also began with a birdie putt from much closer range. Lee widened the gap to two when, after both finding sand with our second shots, he came out to within a foot for a four against my five. I got one back at the next, which he three putted, but he went two up again at the fifth where he holed from fifteen feet for a birdie four and I missed from twelve feet.

Lee's clowning took him among the crowd at the sixth where he commandeered a soft drink stand for a while and gave away lemonade to the spectators. This sort of thing is typically Trevino and could upset many players, but I have been in situations like this before and have never let his antics upset me. I was, nevertheless, quite happy when I was drawn to play with the more conservative Nicklaus on the last day.

Trevino is much more highly strung than people imagine. The immediate impression is of a powerfully built, happy extrovert determined to squeeze every ounce of fun out of life. A showman supreme and certainly good for the golf game. But his prowling round the green before putting, his continual chatter have their roots in nervous strain, I am sure.

He was unlucky at the sixteenth where a dog barked as he putted but he holed from way beyond the hole at the eighteenth after I had pitched dead, finishing in seventy-two, against my seventy-three. With a round to go I was alongside Nicklaus and Sanders on 210 with Trevino on 208 and looking very much a winner. It had been quite a day and I joined in the laughter as Lee gagged his way through a joint press conference. Some of his cracks are a little frayed (like the one about his wife still having the same milkman although the family home has been moved 480 miles) but he is an engaging character who does all sorts of nice things for people. But as I have said, there was no pain for me in the switch for the final day which paired Lee and the equally colourful Sanders together, leaving Nicklaus and myself as the straight men in the final act.

I felt completely at home with Jack. I have spent quite a lot of time with him at his home in Florida and under his coaching have come to share his enthusiasm for game fishing and the sea. In golf he is a tremendous technician and loves to talk about technique.

We opened with fours but at the next I pulled my second left of the green and pitched twenty feet past. Nicklaus holed from eleven feet for his three to my five but if the crowd sensed that maybe the trophy would be taking its accustomed route across the Atlantic after a short stay here in a bank in Scunthorpe, they did not show it. Rather I felt that they were willing in every putt, urging on every approach shot to the green and if I let them down they can be assured that my disappointment that the putting touch had deserted me was certainly as great as theirs.

We were both short at the long fifth but after pitching twenty feet right of the hole Nicklaus rolled in the putt, I missed from a little longer range so that with thirteen holes to play I was three adrift. From behind came news that Trevino was in trouble but that Sanders had birdied two of the first five holes. On all recent form it seemed impossible that Doug was in with a chance but he had worked harder on his game in recent months than for a very long time and his new mallet headed putter was really hot.

Jack and I took three to get down after both finishing short of the sixth green so that now he was level with Sanders, two shots ahead of Trevino, and three ahead of me. I laid a very long putt dead from the right top edge of the seventh green and felt just a little charge when Nicklaus took three to get down from ten yards but he put things back as they were with a three at the tenth. I needed a few birdies, and quickly, but they did not come and in fact I missed from only two feet at the fifteenth and finished in seventy-six.

Trevino, who had taken forty to the turn and then three putted the eleventh, looked far from the happy bandido of golf as his long cherished hopes disappeared in the wake of fine golf from Sanders and Nicklaus. He holed a great putt on the last hole to finish joint third with Harold Henning on 285, but could not hide his disappointment. He loves the game in this country and says that he will be back every year.

Henning, who now putts cross handed with his left below his right, played remarkably steadily. It was in the end a card player's Open. Nicklaus and Henning are very fine bridge players—the slim South African is I believe up to international standard—and both Trevino and Sanders have been known to take more than a modest swipe at the dealer on the blackjack tables in Las Vegas and London.

Immediately behind me on 287 came Neil Coles and the young giant, Peter Oosterhuis. Neil, a deceptively quiet man in that he is one of the toughest battlers I know, had been having a wonderful season in Britain and Europe and after years of what he admitted had been a negative approach to the Open he prepared really thoroughly for this one. Basically he does not like links courses and is not a good wind player but in finishing only four strokes behind he must surely repeat the thorough build up to the 1970 Open when he goes to Royal Birkdale next year. Both his golf and his temperament have 'Open Winner' written all over them.

Oosterhuis clearly has enormous potential. There are few young players more completely British in their upbringing, schooling and approach to the game. He was still at Dulwich School when he made the Walker Cup side in 1967 and the grin way up there on the peak where his head is still that of a schoolboy enjoying every golfing experience as if for the first time.

He shot on to the scene with sixty-nines in the second and third rounds and must have exceeded his wildest dreams by finishing only four shots back. He hits the ball tremendous distances, but is at times a little wild. Like many big men—Julius Boros and Harry Weetman come to mind—he has a very delicate touch round and on the greens and if he gets a little more accuracy from the tee and more aggression from a hundred yards in I am sure he will be a great player.

Hugh Jackson was on 288. He is a very close friend and

stayed with us at Glamis House. Only recently has he realized how good he is and when we talked about the championship when it was all over we realised that had he not dropped five shots in the first four holes on the last day he would have been in the play-off. After his terrible start he was three under par for the last thirteen, scoring unequalled by anyone for those holes on a day when the delightful John Panton was the only man to better par.

The big surprise was Gary Player's failure to make the last day. Gary had been having a successful time in the U.S. and was second among the money winners behind Trevino, but after a seventy-four and two seventy-fives was one too many. At the Sean Connery pro-am which preceded the Open he had used the cack-handed grip and said then that he believed the majority of players would use this left hand below right style by the time the seventies are out. I appreciate that this method gives a firmer anchor point with the left hand blocking the putter face at the hole but I will have to be quite desperate to change from the conventional method and the hand arrangement we use for all other clubs.

It was, as everyone agreed, a great and financially successful championship. There were long hold-ups at times, particularly at the sixth and twelfth holes which share the same huge green, but it is difficult to see a way round this problem of greens being used for holes both on the way out and way back. But the R. & A. have done a great job in bringing the Open into line with modern day requirements and, with the possible exception of the Masters which has a permanent home at the Augusta National Club, the oldest championship must also rank as the best organised.

Before leaving the scene of Nicklaus's second triumph I must say a word about the crowds in Scotland. I played my first serious golf after my U.S. Open at Troon and St. Andrews and in both places the reception was wonderful. And their knowledge of the game is second to none. As to St. Andrews, the championship has many homes and there is criticism that the old town and the Old Course have been left behind by the talents and equipment of the modern players and the demands of the huge crowds which now watch the Open. Much of the criticism is valid but it would surely be heresy to take St. Andrews off the rota. Practice facilities are limited, the course ridiculously short when conditions are good, but a look at the scores hardly suggests that this finest field of all time set the course ablaze. This may happen on occasions, as it did for a while on the first day, but when affronted in this way the course has a way of calling in aid from the gods and getting the weather it needs to chasten the vandals.

I cannot leave a championship and a town which breathes golf from every pore of its ancient buildings and quaint streets without recalling the first reunion of champions dinner in the R. & A. clubhouse at the beginning of the week. The list was almost complete of former winners still living. . . . Arthur Havers, Gene Sarazen, Dick Burton, Fred Daly, Roberto de Vicenzo, Arnold Palmer, Kel Nagle, Bobby Locke, Henry Cotton, Peter Thomson, Densmore Shute, Bob Charles, Max Faulkner, Jack Nicklaus, Gary Player and myself.

It was an evening of misty-eyed nostalgia for the old timers, fine wine and food. But it did seem a little hard on the new boy among the ex-champs that he was called upon to reply for

the guests on behalf of and in front of such a distinguished
gathering.

For the record, here are the scores of the top twelve in the
1970 championship. I have made it twelve so that I can include
Palmer, the man who pumped life into the Open when he first
came to it in 1960 and set a trend which has been followed by
almost every top American. I had spent a lot of time with
Arnold the previous week, and if the schedule we followed for
T.V. was tough on me, it must have been a killer for him.

283—Jack Nicklaus   (68-69-73-73)   Doug Sanders   (68-71-71-73)
285—Lee Trevino   (68-68-72-77)   Harold Henning (67-72-73-73)
286—Tony Jacklin   (67-70-73-76)
287—Neil Coles   (65-74-72-76)   Peter Oosterhuis (73-69-69-76)
288—Hugh Jackson   (69-72-73-74)
289—John Panton   (72-73-71-71)   Peter Thomson   (68-74-73-74)
      Tommy Horton (66-73-75-75)
290—Arnold Palmer   (68-72-76-74)

III

The Build-up to Two Opens

III

The Build-up to Two Opens

The opening to a 1970 season which brought the unforgettable joy of victory at Chaska and the disappointment of defeat behind Jack Nicklaus at St. Andrews was, I felt certain, going to be a quiet one as far as my own golf and earnings were concerned. The Weiskopf's had spent their first English Christmas with us at our new house in Elsham and although I felt in good shape mentally I had played little golf and felt that it would be some time before my game became sharp enough to give me a chance in the hottest of all golf schools.

I had not practised in Lincolnshire during my holiday because going out in the cold and rain does more harm to the spirit than any good the swinging may do to one's game. My home parts in winter are for shooting and log fires and plenty of good home-cooking which we miss so much abroad. I am convinced that to practise when it is cold and wet is pointless and in six weeks or so I played only one game at Woodhall Spa, a course owned by stockbroker Neil Hotchkin and one of the finest in the world.

Bradley was still only a few weeks old when I left for Los Angeles and the L.A. Open which has for long been the traditional curtain-raiser on a tour which now boasts a total in prize

Tony, Viv, and the U.S. Open Trophy. For the first time for fifty years, a British player has won the most coveted prize in the world. (F.G.)

U.S. Open, 1970, Round I.

Later, confident, when the short putts are dropping, Jacklin acknowledges the applause, as his other partner, amateur Steve Melnik, prepares to putt. (F.G.)

On the first tee, pensive, with playing partner Billy Casper and *Financial Times* golf correspondent, Ben Wright. (F.G.)

U.S. Open, Round II.
One of the most anxious moments of the Championship. On the edge of the eighteenth green, there is some doubt as to whether a spectator or Jacklin's caddie had inadvertently kicked Tony's ball. Finally, the referee agreed that the ball was kicked by the spectator. (F.G.)

U.S. Open, Round III.
The half-way leader driving. (F.G.)

Toward the end of Round III, Jacklin putts, as the fiery,
ever-on-the-move Dave Hill, looks on. (F.G.)

Tony, really tense, looks mystified as a putt slips by the hole. (F.G.)

U.S. Open, Round IV.
The moment of triumph. The champion, at the presentation,
makes his victory speech. (F.G.)

Back home, the holder of the British and U.S. Open Championships is introduced to the Prime Minister, Mr. Edward Heath, by Mr. William Whitelaw, captain of the Royal and Ancient. (F.G.)

Emotionally drained, Jacklin is interviewed by the Press after his
remarkable first round has been rained off. (F.G.)

The British Open, 1970.
In Round IV, Jacklin and the American, Lee Trevino, enjoy a drink. (C.S.)

money of seven million dollars. Arnold Palmer, who has made a close study of these things, believes that in the next five years this sum will rise to ten million, at which point, he suggests, the figure will peg itself, the calendar being full, and the sponsors committed to the limit.

From the sidelines golf might appear to concern the top twenty or so players jetting in and out of cities, picking up huge cheques, retreating to their homes and boats and attending the business meetings which have become a necessary part of their way of life. Palmer and Nicklaus have their own jets, Nicklaus has a boat or two, Casper lives in a mansion with his eight children (three of his own and five more adopted) and Sanders and Trevino have built pads worth 200,000 dollars or so.

But the tour is tough and the tension great. The weeks follow a similar pattern—travel Monday, practice or rest Tuesday, a pro-am on Wednesday, then the four days of the tournament. The Australian Bruce Crampton once kept up this punishing schedule for 48 weeks in a year and many players compete in more than forty events annually. It was onto this scene of riches and ulcers and tranquillisers that I walked as British Open champion at the beginning of 1970.

After winning at Royal Lytham from Bob Charles six months earlier I had said that the next phase in my career was to establish myself as a personality and a winner in America. I had won the Jacksonville Open at the beginning of 1968 but this was not enough to mean much in the land of the Big Three and all the other great stars and to get my face on the front of the magazines. I knew that I had a long way to go. It is one thing to want to be the best golfer in the world, and I have always wanted to be that, and another to achieve it.

J.—5

I played in the Bing Crosby and that is as far as it went. I have never known anyone so completely like his screen self as Bing and I was thrilled to get a telegram from him after the U.S. Open.

Towards the end of the Crosby I began to feel a little more confident but I was still, in my view, far from fully wound up when the highly paid battalions moved on to San Diego for the Andy Williams Classic.

I surprised myself with an opening sixty-six for the lead and followed this with a sixty-seven. Although I was still in front after a third round seventy-one I slipped in the last round and with an amazing last nine Pete Brown came through the field to catch me and tie on 275. Brown's game was still sizzling, mine now not as sharp as it had been, and at the first hole of the play-off I pushed my tee-shot into the trees. It was impossible to reach the green with my second and Pete, playing the hole perfectly, had a par four to my five to snatch first prize, and had to settle for second place and 17,100 dollars. Quite a nice sum to settle for but I should have won.

It would probably have been better had I stayed with the tour but I had already arranged to fly home for the christening of Bradley Mark—names on which Viv and I had stumbled and not after anyone in particular—and the trip to Buckingham Palace to receive my O.B.E. The ceremony was most impressive and I felt thrilled to be there; but what happened when I came out of the palace had me in a terrible flap.

Eamonn Andrews was outside the gates and I was whisked into a car and off to the B.B.C. studios. He has been associated with sports as well as other programmes for a long while and

I thought he wanted to interview me about the presentation and golf. He did, in a way, but on the 'This is Your Life' programme. Family and friends had known about this for some time but Sarah Chappell, the public relations girl who works for Mark McCormack in London, had actually fixed appointments that afternoon for me so that I would not suspect anything.

Bill Shankland, who did so much to knock off the rough edges of an ambitious, brash Lincolnshire kid at Potters Bar, was there but the biggest surprise came when Bert Yancey walked on. He had been flown from America and after the show flew straight back. I remember now that the day before I was doing some work on this book and my mother made a great fuss about my getting some new shoes . . . I had taken only one pair to London and black socks for the O.B.E. ceremony and my saying, 'Heck, mother, the Queen won't spend all afternoon looking at my feet.' No doubt mother wanted me to look right for the telly, but how they kept the secret I'll never know.

My two-week holiday had proved to be as hectic as any spell on the U.S. tour. The day after 'This is Your Life' I was on the train to Tilbury to see some shoe people about a contract but after three meetings in London later that day I managed to escape back to Elsham for a short break before going to Doral in Florida. I had missed Viv and the baby a lot in January and we all went to America this time. What holds one about a kid who sleeps most of the time and cannot say a thing I cannot say but I had decided after a month on my own on the West Coast that Master B. M. Jacklin would be a flying veteran by the time he was a year old.

At Doral I played quite well and with rounds of seventy-seventy-two-seventy-three-seventy-four finished joint eighth on 289, ten shots behind the winner Mike Hill but a satisfactory start after two weeks without any sort of golf. The Florida courses are all very much the same but golf there is enjoyable and after failing to make the cut in the Citrus Invitation at Orlando I finished joint fourth at Pensacola. I was happy with my game there, for Pensacola is far from my favourite course, and I actually had a chance of winning after a third round sixty-six which included six birdies and an eagle.

I will always have a soft spot for Jacksonville having broken the ice there in 1968 and the improvement I had shown at Pensacola continued. I began with a seventy, followed it with a brace of two seventy-twos, but then played as well as I can for a sixty-seven which put me in third place behind Don January, who tied with Dale Douglas and won the play off. The cash at Jacksonville put me in the top ten money winners' list for the first time and when we began at Miami in the National Airlines tournament I was in fifth place. It had always been my ambition to establish myself in the top ten . . . as in pop music, being in the charts is all-important to us.

I knew after a first-round seventy-five that I would have to break seventy in the second round and I looked like doing it in this chase for a first prize of 40,000 dollars until the sixteenth, where I hooked my tee shot a few yards out of bounds, took seven and failed to make the last two days. I had intended following the Nicklaus routine of skipping Greensboro so that I could give myself a full week's preparation at Augusta National before the Masters but after my flop at Miami I decided that with a wife and now a family to support I would go to Greensboro for a little more bread. Play was washed out the first day, which was particularly tough on Palmer and Casper. They had been invited to a dinner at the White House given for the Duke and Duchess of Windsor and although scheduled for two rounds on the Sunday both went through with an engagement which meant almost non-stop plane hopping and car dashes between the second and third rounds. Arnold was the surprise leader on 131 before the whirlwind travelling and high-powered socialising began but he faded badly over the last thirty-six after so little sleep and Player won on 271. I performed reasonably but the putting worries which were to bother me until Chaska made themselves felt and I finished eight shots behind Gary.

The Masters at Augusta was the brainchild of the great Bobby Jones and Cliff Roberts, a stockbroker who now keeps an eye on one of the world's greatest tournaments from his cabin at the end of the clubhouse verandah. It is his practice to call players in from time to time and such a call is treated by the recipient as a royal command. Mr. Roberts is immensely proud of his tournament and in the face of pressure to change the system of invitations has said that the Masters will be run in its present form or not at all.

Although leading the money winners at the time Trevino refused to play in the 1970 Masters and in a not so silent protest argued that places in the field were going to amateurs and players from other countries who were not worthy of a spot at Augusta but were qualifying through an outdated system of invitations. Lee made his point and stayed home but the Masters went on as usual with its customary vast crowds; and since the event is run by a private club if Trevino is to play in the future he will have to change his views about the Masters. The Augusta National appears to be quite happy with things as they are, and not in the mood to listen to demands that the first sixty on the tour the previous year be invited automatically. 'They are out of step,' bellowed Trevino. To which Augusta officials replied that they saw no particular reason why they be in step with anyone else in view of the great success of their tournament and the high esteem in which it was held throughout the world.

This was my fourth Masters and I felt that my general form of recent weeks entitled me to feel that I had a chance. I fell in love with this beautifully laid out course when I first saw it after Neil Coles had turned down an invitation to play there in 1967. Neil hates flying and although only twenty-two I jumped at the chance and spent the first few hours of that initial Georgia stay recovering from the splendour of it all. Someone told me then that the water in the lakes was dyed blue and the grass a brighter green because of coloured television but I could not believe it. Surely no one would take such liberties at Augusta. But they did, and still do. Next time I went there I felt like plucking at the azaleas and dogwood to make sure they were real. Of course they are, but many are planted just before the tournament to make it look at its magnificent best during the week of the big show.

Those champions, like Palmer and Nicklaus, who between them have worn the coveted green blazer at the victory ceremony on seven occasions, will tell you that the course never comes up the same two years running. This time those who plot some new little mischief through the summer and autumn months when the course is closed had moved the trap on the right of the first fairway nearer the hole to prevent the big hitters flying it from the tee and had made two mounds along the right side of the fifteenth fairway. The area where the mounds have been placed was one from which long hitters could carry the water and hit the green in two, and in spite of the bumps a great number of players played the hole as a par four.

I was heading for a seventy-one in the first round when at the eighteenth my tee shot caught the trees on the right and finished in real trouble. I tried to clear the tree trunks in front of me, but caught the very last of them and bounced out on to the tenth fairway. From there I had a shot over a scoreboard and my ball finished through the back of the green. Three to get down from there and my seventy-one became a seventy-three. Next day I played some of the worst golf of my life, had three sixes yet somehow escaped with a seventy-four and qualified for the last two days. I had more luck in that round than I had known all season, but in the next two days the longest putt I holed was from fifteen feet and my total of 288 gave me the highest ever finish by a Briton. I was joint twelfth but nine shots behind the winner.

Casper, who had thrown away a wonderful victory chance the previous year, tied with Gene Littler on 279 after a putt for outright victory had literally gone into the hole and out again. Billy and Gene, who played together as youngsters back home in California, both wanted a first Masters blazer badly but Casper, at one time eight ahead, came home an easy winner.

Littler rebuilds vintage cars in his spare time and Casper is a devout Mormon who takes weeks away from the tour to visit U.S. troops and do church work. They are both delightful people, with two of the finest swings in golf, but by nature a long way removed from the popular image of the swinging, live-it-up-type tour pro. In fact there are not so many of the latter around these days. Ray Floyd still likes to get home with the milk, but Mrs. Scotty Sanders seems to have done a fine job in taming her old fireball.

My father was with me at the Masters, and from Augusta we went to Atlanta to link up with some of the family. We had all planned a week's break at Sea Island, the club I represent on the tour, and had quite a houseful with mum and dad, Viv and Bradley, my sister Lynn, her husband Bob Cranidge and their two children Darran and Lisa. Ken Bowden, editorial director of *Golf Digest*, and my good friend Jack Wood came down for a few days. Jack spent much of his time trying to persuade me to come out of the pool or sea and do some tapeing for the book, but in one day after swimming and golf I managed to persuade him to come horse riding. Rumour has it that he has still not forgiven me, and certainly the only horses he mentions now are things ridden by Piggott.

We swam in the evenings in Hughie Johnson's pool. A Welshman who made his fortune on Wall Street, Hughie and his wife Alice live at Sea Island for five months a year and although in their sixties both play golf and swim every day. We are having a two-bedroom apartment built at Sea Island, a wonderful spot which has all the elegance and calm of Scotland's Gleneagles.

Vivien and I left the family at Sea Island and went to La Costa for the Tournament of Champions. I played well and after rounds of sixty-nine-sixty-eight-sixty-seven was two behind the leader Frank Beard. I then made one of those mistakes which infuriate me. The clock goes on an hour in that part of the U.S. on the night of April 26 and I forgot to put the hands forward. I was sitting in the clubhouse talking to Frank Sinatra's agent over a coffee when someone came in and said my caddy was going mad. I thought I had an hour and ten minutes to spare, but realising what had happened I hustled on to the tee and without any practice bogeyed the first hole with a five and never properly settled down. I am not saying that I would have won, for Frank Beard paralysed the field by seven shots, but my seventy-six was a lot worse than the previous rounds and I finished joint third with Casper and Player.

The run-up to the U.S. Open from La Costa was not too rewarding either for my morale or my bank balance. I made the last day in the Atlanta Classic and a few hundred dollars, missed the cut in the Memphis Open on the sort of course I dislike . . . short, too many out of bounds, and small greens. At Quail Hollow, Kemper, I had an agonising week on the greens and I again putted badly in the Western Open in Chicago.

And so to Minneapolis, and the Hazeltine National Golf Club. The cracks about Hazeltine dropped as thick as the bogeys shot by the big names :—

'Let's rent an electric reaper and play a quick eighteen.'

'Are the greens mowed and the automatic milking machines working?'

'Even the locker room has a dog-leg.'

'I'd withdraw but I don't know how to get back to town.'

But I would have happily made my last journey back from beautiful Hazeltine on an electric reaper, or on the back of one of Dave Hill's cows.

It was not until we flew in to Heathrow that I was fully aware of the impact my victory at Chaska had made in Britain. The last day of the U.S. Open coincided with the final of the

World Cup in Mexico City and perhaps disappointed soccer fans found in my win in foreign fields some consolation. There was one amusing moment in a T.V. interview when the interviewer said that he imagined I had felt fairly confident before putting on the last green. I'll say I did having seven putts from thirty feet for the title.

Before leaving for America seven weeks earlier I had promised my old school master Mr. Driskell that I would present the prizes at a sports day in Scunthorpe and this meant driving straight up to Lincolnshire. The kids gave me a terrific reception and somehow this was among the most warming of the many nice things which happened at that time.

The following day Viv and I drove in Scunthorpe's equivalent of a motorcade to a reception given by the Mayor and for the rest of the week I took what chances I had of resting because I knew that from the following Monday almost every minute of the next fifteen days had been planned for me. And, as an example of the kind of pressures we sometimes have to face, they are worth describing in quite some detail.

On Monday, I flew from Kinnington Aerodrome near my home at Elsham at 7.30 a.m. across the Humber to Brough, changed planes there and flew to Watford and from there by car to Sunningdale for a morning clinic and afternoon match with that remarkable amateur Michael Bonallack. Mike is perhaps the greatest British amateur of all times and certainly one of sport's nicest people. He is big, ambling, completely unspoilt and from 100 yards is one of the best players, amateur or professional, in the world. Add to this a really sound long game on which ace teacher Leslie King has worked so hard, and one cannot be surprised by his unrivalled success.

The day was put on by Colgate-Palmolive with whom I have contracts. The clinic went well and although this was supposed to be a private day hundreds of people who had no connection with the firm were out on one of Britain's most beautiful courses. This was the first time I had played since Chaska and I was beaten by five shots—Bonallack going round in sixty-nine. I did not play all that well and had not anticipated that I would, but Mike, who drapes himself over his putter and hits the ball halfway up giving it a lot of top spin, can be absolutely deadly. I was still winding down but knew that I would have to crank up quickly for the T.V. series with Palmer, other T.V. matches, the Sean Connery Pro-Am at Troon and the defence of my Open title. Flying down to Watford that morning I thought how nice it would be if the pilot headed south round London and flew me down for some sun in Spain or Portugal.

After the match I took a car to London Airport and caught the 7.30 plane to Manchester, from there to Southport, dinner with Arnold and his family, a briefing by producer Phil Pilley and bed.

The holes played are described as the best eighteen holes in Britain. As people will no doubt point out they are nothing of the sort but they were the eighteen best holes we had time to play. Without doing a commercial for the series, however, I will say that the producer sorted out some of the toughest and most terrifying holes I know, and those who are familiar with the courses on which we did the filming will appreciate this point as I go through the period day by day.

The fact that no courses south of Hoylake, near Liverpool, were used will no doubt bring protest from readers and viewers, but Pilley always stands to be shot at. It is impossible to name any eighteen holes as the best in Britain for one could shoot a dozen such matches and not duplicate one hole. The idea is a good one and maybe one day we will have the time to play a more representative selection.

Members of the various clubs had been told in advance that we would be playing their courses and most days there were upwards of 2,000 people present to see the great old champ Arnold and myself playing a hole or two. Early on the first morning we played two of Birkdale's long distance holes, the sixth and the fifteenth. Conditions were not good and it was impossible to get up in two at either of them. I cannot give any details of how the match went at the time of writing but the series, the first of its kind shot here, is being shown by the B.B.C. in the spring of 1971.

From Birkdale we went south to Hoylake and played the first and seventh and after a car dash north along the coast the seventeenth at Royal Lytham. This is a hole on which Bobby Jones made four after hitting a long iron from a bunker to within a foot of the pin. A plaque to commemorate one of golf's most talked-of shots is still in that trap and will undoubtedly stay there as long as golf is played at Royal Lytham. We played this hole in driving rain. Still in our soaked waterproofs Arnold and I flew to Prestwick and anyone listening to our conversation would have been left in no doubt how we felt about the conditions and punishingly tight schedule. We stayed the night at Turnberry and the next morning played the seventh and eleventh holes at Troon. The seventh is the famous postage stamp short hole with the rolling green and fierce bunkers at one side, where tens are not unknown, and at the eleventh Nicklaus scored ten during the 1962 Open won by Arnold

Palmer. The conditions were again very rough for these opening holes in Scotland and I needed a four iron at the postage stamp. These two holes can seldom have played harder.

We then went to Prestwick and played the fifteenth but it was now raining so hard that it was decided to abandon filming for the day.

I wanted to get to St. Andrews for some practice on a course on which I had played only two rounds in my career. We were driving in a huge limousine and going through Glasgow, and the chauffeur seemed a little startled when I asked him to stop at a fish and chip shop. Willie my caddy nipped in and got three papers of haddock and chips and we pulled into a side road and ate them. This was just about the most relaxing moment of that fortnight.

We played a practice round on the Old Course on Thursday . . . Nicklaus and Trevino were already there . . . then back to Turnberry on Friday to play the ninth and fifteenth for the T.V. match. A near-gale was blowing and again you would hardly have described Arnold and myself as the happiest golfers in the world. Then it was time for socialising in connection with the Sean Connery Tournament and we went to cocktail parties at Culzean Castle and the Caledonian Hotel in Ayr. The Connery was a huge success particularly for Christy O'Connor who in this friendly prelude to the sterner golfing test to come picked up £2,250. On the Sunday evening we made the long drive to Dundee, and next morning flew in a tiny private plane to play the ninth at Muirfield and the third at North Berwick. There was not room in the plane for our clubs and a baggage wagon followed us round to Muirfield and North Berwick and then on to St. Andrews for what was for me a last practice round before the Open. I was quite happy to rest and leave practice to the other fellows on the eve of the all-important Championship.

On the Sunday of the play-off between Nicklaus and Sanders, with our thoughts still very much at St. Andrews, Palmer and I were out filming again. We left at six o'clock in the morning for Carnoustie where we played the third, sixth, sixteenth and seventeenth and the following day the eleventh, fourteenth, and seventeenth at St. Andrews. That afternoon I played an eighteen-hole match against Gay Brewer and, after doing some work on a T.V. commercial, Viv and I at last drove home to Elsham. Our house there, East Lodge, has never looked better. There was a huge pile of mail and among the many letters I will treasure was one from the Duke of Windsor. It was written from the liner, *Michelangelo*, and the Duke wrote how, as a keen golfer, he had been thrilled by my victory in the U.S. Open. He added that he hoped we would meet one day so that I could give him my own account of Hazeltine. This I certainly hope to do. Another letter was from an eighty-seven-year-old Scot enclosing a booklet entitled *How to play the Old Course*. It was written in 1930 and no doubt on winter evenings in the future I will flick through it, recall that opening twenty-nine for the outward half, and the monsoon, and wonder whether the weather robbed me of a second win in the British Open.

I had arranged to play with Bert Yancey in the Laurel Valley Foursomes and the Westchester Classic but after a few days at home realised that I was still not ready for serious golf. I did some rough shooting and Viv and I thoroughly enjoyed having friends in for dinner. She has become a wonderful cook, and I have developed quite a taste for good wine.

I felt that we both needed a holiday and a crowd of us from the Scunthorpe area went down to Penina in Portugal where Henry Cotton and his wife now live.

We played golf with Henry and in the evenings he took us out to some small but marvellous restaurants where we had the best sea food I have ever eaten. Henry and Toots are marvellous hosts and if this is the way old champions live I will not be too upset when my time comes. But hopefully, that is a long way off.

We came back after ten days of living in a temperature consistently in the mid-eighties and it was time to go back to the United States. I had re-charged the batteries and now looked forward to big time golf again. Although it meant letting some people down I could not possibly have gone back any earlier and Bert Yancey had set my mind at rest, having been kind enough to telephone and say that although my withdrawal meant a last minute search for a new partner, he fully understood.

IV

The Beginnings

IV

The Beginnings

The beginnings were humble and our working class background in Scunthorpe was hardly the sort from which golfers sprang in the forties and fifties. My father had a number of jobs in those days, driving a locomotive in the local steel works, then a lorry, and then for a couple of years when I was quite young he ran a fish and chip shop at Winteringham, a village some eight miles from Scunthorpe.

I was born at number forty-four Henderson Avenue but before I went away to Potters Bar to begin my career in golf under Bill Shankland I had lived in seven different houses. There must have been a little of the gypsy spirit in the Jacklin family and maybe this constant moving stood me in good stead later in life. The professional golfer is something of a nomad and I would never have had what success has been mine had I not been quite happy travelling about the world living out of a suitcase, pitching the family tent in strange towns and cities week after week.

My mother, Doris, had a good voice and sang with local amateur operatic societies, but undoubtedly the great character of the family was old David Jacklin, my grandfather. In all my travels I have never met anyone quite like him and I often tell people that they have missed something in life if they haven't met my grand-dad. He was a docker at Immingham and by all accounts had a fantastic appetite for work. Deep down I know he is proud of what I have done but as we say in the North of England he never lets on that there is anything particularly special about having a grandson who has made a name for himself in world golf. Now eighty, he still rides a motorbike and rides to his various gardening jobs on the old machine. Arthur, my dad, inherited a lot of his father's independence and spirit. He loves to tell the story of the donkey he looked after one winter for a man who gave children rides at one of the nearby seaside towns. He took the animal to school with him one day, tethered it to the railings outside, but was sent home at lunchtime leading it by a piece of string having been told by the teacher that donkeys were all right on the sands at Cleethorpes but could not be brought to school.

I went to the Henderson Avenue infant school and the Doncaster Road secondary school. I was in the 'A' grade at Doncaster Road but never really liked school and the happiest day I spent there was my last one. I have often heard that one's school days are the happiest of one's life but I hated most of them and left as soon as I could when I was fifteen. I was competent at maths and usually came top in P.T. and carpentry. I used to make stools and tables and at my parents' home a table I made at Doncaster Road is still in the lounge. I also enjoyed art and poetry but can never claim to have been much of a scholar. I was into every bit of mischief going but was never happier than when playing games. I played soccer as a half-back but moved up to inside-forward in the school team, and thought at the time that I would like to become a professional footballer. But once I was bitten by the mysteries and challenges of golf I knew that this was the game for me. Injuries from playing football meant that I could not go down to the Scunthorpe Golf Club and practice, so I soon decided to give up all other sports and concentrate on golf. It was a happy decision.

We have always been a closely knit family and I am lucky in having a really wonderful sister, Lynn. She is a couple of years older and always looked after me in the way older sisters do. We went most places together and one of the few bad spots of bother we got into came when we spent our bus fare to Sunday school on sweets. We went home and said that we had been down to the church hall but parents have a way of finding things out and for a while Lynn and I were made to walk to the school on Sundays without the option of swapping our fare for a bag of sweets. Sunday school used to seem a waste of time; and although I believe in God, I seldom go to church although Vivien did drag me there on Father's Day in the U.S. a couple of years ago.

Round about the time I started golf Lynn won a silver medal at her school's music festival, but she was always domestically minded and is happily married to a good chum of mine Bob Cranidge. Darran, their son, hits a fair ball for a three-year-old and their daughter Lisa is about the same age as our boy Bradley.

My dad took up golf late in life and I often wonder if I would have become interested had he not done so. A lot of the lads at school played cricket but I always found the game a complete bore. I think I have only held a bat five times in my life and I will not lose any sleep if I never pick up another one.

I was eleven when I started caddying at Scunthorpe Golf Club for my father and after he had played he would give me an old cut-down ladies three wood and let me hit a ball or two. The members at Scunthorpe were always most encouraging. It mattered not that my environment in a game always associated with people who drove motor cars, not lorries, was against this early start, and I can never thank them enough for their help.

Today things have changed. The achievements of men like Palmer, Player, Nicklaus and Casper have done a tremendous amount to popularise golf and because of the game's acceptance as a sport for everyone it has become much more democratic.

Golf got little space in newspapers when I was a kid and there was little television to bring the great players and great matches into our homes. Now it is reported fully and has changed from being a game for those with money. Tens of thousands are finding each year that it is no longer a rich man's game, and discovering the joy of five-mile hikes with some real purpose to them. Any kid with ambition can build up a set of clubs, and through the English Golf Union and other organisations, coaching is given on a massive scale.

I was always a stubbornly independent kid and to pay for my equipment and golf did a paper round. After the round I would go to the Appleby Frodingham Steel Works and sell papers at the gates to the grey-looking men in flat caps with often just a bare collar stud where richer folk wear ties. Often these bluff characters who sweated through their day in the fiercest of heat told me that I would be mad to follow them into the works which provided employment for so many of the local population.

Saturday mornings I had another job, and this one gave me much more fun than the paper round. In Scunthorpe market

one of those quick-fire salesmen who brighten up such scenes
with their marvellous patter took me on his 'staff'. I used to
hand him up sheets and towels and teacloths which he sold at
'knock-down' prices, and occasionally, when his voice got hoarse
and his larynx in need of lubrication at the nearest pub, I took
over the selling.

Hard work is, of course, the secret of all successful games
players and for months after joining the club as a junior member I plugged away, regularly breaking 100 but never getting
lower than ninety-two. My first target was a series of humps
some 160 yards down the first fairway and when I could make
this regularly I began to go round the course.

The first break-through after what seemed years without
much progress came one day when I shot an eighty-four but any
cockiness that I may have felt about this was knocked out of
me in the next six months during which I regularly failed to
repeat that figure.

I used to get a little despondent, but then there would again
be sudden improvement, and I remember my excitement when
I broke eighty for the first time. I had a longish handicap and
from it won the first four club competitions in which I played.
I was by far the youngest player in the club, not yet fourteen,
and in my first 'away' tournament at Elsham where we now
live I did the last nine holes in par figures for a nett sixty-three.

I was now ready for the Lincolnshire Boys' Championship.
It was played over my own course and after a disheartening
eighty-one in the first round I shot a sixty-six to break both the
professional and amateur records. When I left school I started
work as an apprentice fitter in the steel works for a wage of
£3 11s. 3d. a week and although after a year I went to work

for a solicitor I knew in my heart that the only job in which I would ever be really interested was that of a golfer.

I began playing at Holme Hall where there were a number of low handicap players and after a while decided to rig up my own practice net in our tiny back yard. It consisted of an asbestos sheet and because there was not enough money in the Jacklin golf fund to buy too many balls I used little chunks of rubber cut off an old garden hose. The light evenings were played out to the background of this din as chunks of hard rubber crashed against the asbestos and the neighbours must have thought that Mrs. Jacklin's tubby little lad, Tony, had gone mad.

Without doubt the basis of my game had been formed during my school holidays. After the paper round I would collect a loaf, some butter and jam or cheese from home and cycle off to the course. My parents did not see me until it was dark. Maybe that is why, when I win something these days they always say, 'Well done son, you've earned it.' They are thinking back to those early mornings, the steel works, the madness in the back yard and twelve-hour days at the club where I would help the greenkeeper in the mornings in exchange for an old ball or two, practise in the afternoons and in the summer months persuade members that I was worth playing with when they arrived at the club from work.

Because I wanted so badly the money to be a golfer I suppose I was a bit of a scrounger. The Woodbine cigarettes which most people smoked round our way were ninepence for five and definitely out of my reach. I used to buy cigarette papers and collect the tab ends from the ash trays in the club. Yet in spite of the lengths I went to in those days for a smoke I have never been hooked. I now have two or three in the evening and often give them up for months. And then I used to find quite a lot of balls on the course, but since losing one seemed a major crime I sold them to members and used the money for my bus fares to local competitions.

I was seldom off the course and maybe sometimes a little precocious and a nuisance. This was certainly so one Sunday morning when I was practicing chipping from a spot not far from the bar window. The captain and members were all strengthening their golf muscles in the traditional steel town way of lifting pints and what I hoped was a delicate little shot came too quickly off the club and smashed through the window. I was used to a certain amount of strong language but the things the captain, Jack Webster, said to me after that rude interruption of a Sunday morning ritual had me in tears.

Had my parents been well off I would, I suppose, have taken the fashionable amateur route to the top or wherever it was I was going. I played for both the English and British boys' sides but there was not a ghost of a chance of my being able to afford to play in the long chain of events which make up the amateur season. I have never felt that my golf suffered because of this lack of teenage opportunity. I knew that I was developing a good swing and the fact that I could only play locally made me determined to build up my game and one day make the grade. Today the accepted procedure is to make a name as an amateur before turning professional. Palmer and Nicklaus did this in the fifties and early sixties and almost every top class young amateur will turn professional. With so much money to be won and earned from endorsements, youngsters feel that they must take the plunge.

I won the Lincolnshire Championship and in November

1961 went with my father to Potters Bar in Hertfordshire for an interview with Bill Shankland, an Australian Rugby League star, and a fine professional. Sam Kennedy, a friend in Scunthorpe, had told us that Mr. Shankland wanted an assistant and although my parents were against the idea I eventually persuaded them that I should at least go down to see what this apprentice's job was all about. Shankland offered me £6 per week plus 50 per cent of any money I could earn from teaching and playing with members.

I needed no persuading to take the job, for £6 per week plus seemed a fortune. A few days later I presented myself at the home of Mrs. Baker, a very kind lady, who put me up for £3 15s. od. a week. My worldly possessions were with me on the doorstep that afternoon, a suit I had bought from an uncle for a fiver, the contents of a suitcase and a set of golf clubs, with which I had won four Lincolnshire Boys' titles and my home county's Open Championship. I had been something of a little tin god around Scunthorpe but Shankland was quick to point out that I was absolutely no different from his other assistants. I needed discipline and under Shanko, as we call him, I certainly got it. After three months at Potters Bar I won the Middlesex Alliance title and felt that I was making the grade. I had always set myself targets as my career progressed through its various stages and this was the first of them after my move south.

There were times when life was heartbreaking—long hours spent practising with Shankland seldom satisfied with what I was doing, cleaning out the shop, travelling to assistants' events by bus with the evenings spent in the digs or at a local cinema. The main line north runs past Potters Bar and often I longed to nip over the fence and hop the train. Maybe that particular train would not be going to Scunthorpe but at least it would be going north and nearer to the folks with whom I had grown up and enjoyed life so much.

I saved like mad and bought my first car, a secondhand Austin A.30. Things were getting a little better and in 1963 I played in my first tournament, the Coxmoor at Wollaton Park, Nottingham. My partner was Eric Lester, for long one of the most amusing and outspoken pros on the British tour and I made the last day. Although I finished fairly well down I won £40 and this seemed an absolute fortune. That year I also played in my first Open Championship and finished twenty-ninth behind Bob Charles who beat Phil Rodgers in a play-off at Royal Lytham and St. Anne's. It was certainly in my mind even then that one day I would win an Open and it was a happy coincidence that I should do so six years later on the course where I made my first appearance.

The members at Potters Bar were delighted with my performance and they told me that I could play in the remaining tournaments that season. The following year I decided to join the tour full-time which meant breaking from Bill Shankland although I was to remain associated with the club. In the winter of 1964 Jack Rubins, the captain of Potters Bar, offered to sponsor me on a trip to South Africa and with the help of £200 given to me by the Dunlop Sports Company I made my first trip outside Britain. I found the greens in South Africa virtually unreadable and when I came back all I had to show for ten weeks' effort was £35 in prize money and a beautiful suntan. If you are a male model or a film star a tan is some sort of currency but looking bronzed is of little help to a golfer if he is skint. In 1965 I was invited to play in the Carling Tournament at PleasantValley, Boston, and by finishing thirty-fourth I won by far the biggest cheque of my career to date, one for 1,000 dollars. I flew straight back from Boston and rang Major John Bywaters of the P.G.A. to ask for a late teeing-off time in the Assistants' Championship at Hartsbourne. After a 4,000-mile journey and practically no sleep I began with a seventy-four, qualified the next evening with a birdie three at the last hole, and then shot two sixty-eights and won the play-off with David Butler and Sean Hunt for my first National title.

My travelling companion in those days was Alex Caygill, a Yorkshireman, who was troubled then by a nervous stomach but who would surely become a player of world class if he would slow down his swing.

While playing in Belfast I met a girl at a dance and stage show in an hotel and dated her a couple of evenings later. I decided then that Vivien, who was working as a punch-card operator in a Belfast office was the girl for me and it has been that way ever since.

We became engaged in November 1965 just before I went to South Africa where I won a tournament at Kimberley and this time showed a considerable profit on the trip. I was writing to Vivien most days and when I came back told her on the telephone that I thought we ought to get married. I was spending a fortune on telephone calls and suggested jokingly that it would be cheaper if we got ourselves to the church, and fast!

We were married at Cooks Centenary Presbyterian Church in May 1966. My family and a number of friends flew over for the ceremony and the same week I won my first tournament, the Blaxnit, in Belfast. Viv had packed in her job a week earlier and it was perhaps an omen for the future that I won on the first occasion on which she walked every round with me. She had never played golf and knew little about this strange game on which her husband-to-be was so crazy, but since then she has plodded round all over the world and been an inspiration in the victories I have gained.

That season I was third in the Penfold, the Agfa and the Martini and I felt sure that I would soon be winning. Viv is a wonderful girl and being married leant very much stronger point to the ambitions I had. After the wedding we had a short honeymoon at Newcastle, Co. Down, which is surely one of the most spectacularly beautiful courses in the world. I now had some real aims in life outside golf for the first time and when I was chosen to play for England in what was then the Canada Cup (now the World Cup) in Tokyo, Viv and I decided to go 'bust' at the bank and have an extended honeymoon in Japan, Australia and the Far East.

I had been to South Africa a couple of times and to Canada but this was a dream-like way of starting off married life and an international career in golf. It was all so much more interesting and rewarding to have Vivien around. We shared wonderful experiences in many places which had been simply strange sounding names for both of us until then and the fact that the bank manager was not over-enthusiastic about this costly trip did not worry us at all. We think very much alike and both of us had an idea that things would soon start happening to the kid from Scunthorpe and his Irish bride.

V

*1967—1969: from Tokyo through Jacksonville
to Royal Lytham*

V

1967–1969: from Tokyo through Jacksonville to Royal Lytham

The trip to Tokyo at the end of 1966 for the World Cup was an exciting one for both Vivien and myself. It was the first time she had made a long flight and I remember we held hands for much of the way—not many newly-married couples can have a working honeymoon to Japan, Australia and the Far East and as well as celebrating our good fortune I was about to play for England for the first time.

Tokyo is a startling place, masses of factories, neon lights, skyscrapers and millions of people. In the World Cup I played against Palmer, an unforgettable experience for someone who had yet to win a major tournament on the British tour. I had won the Blaxnit and been third three times but in big events I had still to break my duck. Now in a country which had always intrigued me I was playing with Peter Allis against Palmer and Nicklaus, a quite frightening experience because Palmer was—well—a god to me and Nicklaus also belonged in the heavens.

I thought, no, I knew that Arnold was the greatest golfer in the world and apart from that he was my image of how the greatest golfer in the world should be, the way he carried himself and everything about him. I was there in this strange land playing against him and it was quite unhinging. I played quite well although Peter and I never threatened to challenge the superiority of these two great Americans; but I did not putt well and I had the feeling when I was playing with Arnold that people weren't really interested in what I was doing. I was sort of putting quickly to get out of the way because I felt that the huge crowds only wanted to watch him and his partner. It was not his fault for he did nothing to cause it, but he has this magic and people respond to it.

After the World Cup we went down to Australia, New Zealand and then up through the Far East. I won the New Zealand P.G.A. Championship, my first victory overseas, and finished third in a tournament in Bangkok. The air fares came to £2,000 and we just about met expenses. In a way it was a free trip but I never looked at it in this way because I was gaining experience and in doing so furthering my golfing education. I had a lot to learn and there was only one way of doing it—to pitch in there, to do my best and learn to ride the bad times of which there were many. The life of the modern golf professional is essentially that of a world traveller and he must learn to adapt. There were many times during that long tour when things were going wrong and both Vivien and I would have given anything to come home. But, for example, from watching Japanese and Chinese players executing bunker shots almost perfectly but taking very little sand, I was able to experiment successfully with my own method.

I played in my first Masters in the spring of 1967, and was drawn with Palmer and shall never forget the reception I was given as I walked up the eighteenth hole. The gallery was made up almost exclusively of Arnie's army but in the second round I shot a seventy against his seventy-three and the wonderful Augusta crowds seemed delighted that I had played so well. The little guy had out-shot the legendary hero of four Masters victories and as sports crowds so often do the people there enjoyed the experience. I have always reacted well to applause . . . maybe my mother being a bit of a star in local music shows had something to do with that . . . but my game and my temperament were not yet ready for such an occasion.

I led for a while in the third round but everything was too much for me and I eventually finished twenty-fifth. But to win a Masters will always remain one of my greatest ambitions.

In spite of my lowly position after being in the fighting line for so long, my performance was regarded as some sort of minor triumph at home. We had been reared in the belief that the Americans were some sort of golfing supermen and I had stayed alongside the greats for a while. However, when I got back home, I could do little right at first and seemed unable to recapture the power or the putting touch which I had enjoyed overseas. Jacko was having a bad time and as so often happens a number of people said that they were not surprised. There was a feeling then that the twenty-two year old from Scunthorpe had set his sights too high.

I began to play better and at last won a tournament, the Pringle at Royal Lytham. My start there was not exactly promising for I began with a seventy-five but followed it with a seventy and made the cut. In the third round a sixty-eight enabled me to pull back five shots on David Snell so that with a round to go I was only one behind. Over the early holes in the afternoon I did not play well and when I took seven at the sixth

I appeared to have little chance. Tony Grubb, Tommy Horton, Dave Thomas were all challenging Snell but after a twenty-foot putt for a birdie three at the eighth and a par three at the ninth, five of us were level. I had another birdie three at the tenth, holed from eight yards for a three at the fifteenth and came back in thirty-two to win by four shots from Snell. A first prize in England at last and the £750 was doubly welcome as that night I flew to Canada, having decided to compete in the Canadian Open. My form improved a lot and tenth place earned me 4,000 dollars.

This was the year remembered warmly by British golf fans for Roberto de Vicenzo's Open victory at Hoylake. He had been near so often but before the championship he said that now he was getting old he had come to Britain to see friends. He made thousands of new ones and few Open winners have known the reception given to Roberto as he walked with that huge smile along the fairway and on to the green at the seventy-second hole. Nicklaus was second, Clive Clark and Gary Player joint third and I was next. Delighted that two young Englishmen had finished so high, Roberto said at the presentation that he hoped that if he could not retain the trophy himself the following year he would have the joy of handing it over to a young British player. I am sure that this wonderful old campaigner did not regret having to wait an extra year for this to happen.

I was now determined to gain as much experience as I could and after the Open flew to New York for the Westchester Classic. It was there that I received a call from McCormack suggesting that I might join him and after a number of talks it was agreed that I would become a member of an organisation which included Palmer, Nicklaus, Player, Sanders, Charles and a number of others. Fred Corcoran, one of sports great impressarios who had managed Babe Ruth, Sam Snead, de Vicenzo and Tony Lema, also had talks with me at that time but I decided to go with Mark. I played in three tournaments without boosting either my bank balance or my confidence and came back early in September. McCormack held a press conference in the Carlton Towers Hotel, London, and announced that he was to be my manager.

I attended this meeting on my way to Sandwich for the Dunlop Masters at Royal St. George's. I was glad to be home again after a disappointing time in America and by the end of the week had won my second home tournament. I began with a sixty-nine, followed it with a very patchy seventy-four but on the last day had rounds of sixty-seven and sixty-four to win. The third round sixty-seven put me in a handy position and the sixty-four not only brought victory but a course record. Henry Cotton had shot a sixty-five in winning his first Open over the Kent course in 1934 and to commemorate his record sixty-five the Dunlop Company named their ball after him, and the Dunlop sixty-five remains one of the world's most famous balls. At the sixteenth in the last round I holed in one—the first ace to be screened live, I believe. I felt after this victory that I had done enough to warrant taking the plunge as a full-time player on the U.S. tour. Earlier that year some people had been amused by my statement that I wanted to be the best player in the world, but I knew that to have any chance of achieving this I had to move on. I had achieved one of my goals by winning twice that year and I was now ready to look at other targets.

I have always had this masochistic thing of wanting to get my brains beaten out in better company. As a boy of twelve and thirteen at Scunthorpe I kept wanting to beat figures like eighty-four and seventy-nine for a round and then because there were no players with a handicap of less than seven at the club I joined a second club, Holme Hall just outside Scunthorpe where they had better players. I reasoned that I would not learn much if I continued to play all my golf at the Scunthorpe club and it was after I had become one of the best players at Holme Hall and won Lincolnshire titles that I moved to Potters Bar. And after winning the Middlesex Alliance Championship I decided to become a playing professional. Now, as I say, I had won twice in Britain and wanted to move on again. Malcolm Gregson, with a series of last round challenges, won three times that year and took the Vardon trophy. He also went to the U.S. but after some back trouble and a lot of bad luck there he has decided that his game is better suited to golf in Britain, South Africa and Australia.

Having decided to play most of the time in the U.S., Vivien and I agreed that in spite of the strangeness of it all we must make ourselves like both the people and their way of life. Neither of us found this at all difficult. Many British people dislike the way Americans express themselves in their talk, in clothes and their motor cars. We liked them immediately, and I became quickly used to the way they cook their steaks and loved their huge sideplates of salad with the wide variety of dressings and admired their enthusiasm for life. Unlike many critics of the American scene I had not been used to the good things and it was probably easier for me to get enthusiastic about living there.

I am sure that coming from life at a place like Scunthorpe, not being an establishment type and used to any particular way of living—helped me to settle down. The new experiences

which came our way almost every day and our determination to
live and work hard among the people who were, after all, our
hosts made this first long trip a happy one.

The first real friends I made among the players were Tom
Weiskopf and Bert Yancey. I think we just met at a tournament
and took a liking to one another. After being out there for a few
weeks Viv and I went to a very swish cocktail party at the
Eldorado Country Club in Palm Springs. There were hundreds
of people there, famous people in sport, local senators, stage and
film stars and the two limeys from across the pond felt distinctly
out of things. Viv and I grabbed a drink each and stood in a
corner talking absolute nonsense to each other, you know, real
gibberish. We just talked away trying to hide the fact that we
felt complete strangers in this rather lush set up. We knew
hardly anyone and it seemed that few people wanted to know
us. Then Ed Furgol, the American pro who reached the top in
spite of his withered arm, invited us to join his friends. After a
while I told him how we felt and he said, 'You wouldn't have
been asked here if you didn't belong here. You've just got to
believe that you do.'

We have been to many of these plush gatherings all over the
world since that night when we were so completely the little boy
and girl lost and enjoyed them. But we are not really cocktail
party types and neither are the Weiskopfs and Yanceys. We all
prefer being with a small crowd but it is impossible not to get
mixed up occasionally in what is a pretty hectic social round. I
am not saying that we intentionally steer clear of a party but we
like to make our own friends.

Life on the American tour can be a continual ball if one wishes
it to be. Invitations pour in all the time but Vivien and I like to

check in at a motel with individual cooking facilities and lead a married life as close to normal as possible. The golf would suffer if we did otherwise.

I remember once in New York a Mr. Richard Widmark telephoned inviting us to stay at his home. He put a whole crowd of us up including Harold Henning and his wife and their two children. Only when we were installed did our host reveal that he and his family were off on vacation and they left us in their fabulous place with maids, cars and everything we wanted. In Palm Springs, George Glickley and his wife Rusty entertained us and at Westchester, Mrs. Sally Francis put us up in her house. From the first time we went there she told us to treat it as home. This sort of thing just happens.

We were at Palm Springs when the McCormack office in Cleveland telephoned to say that I had been booked for a T.V. match in Nairobi. This was again something completely new, a different world. We flew to Africa via London and I think in the early morning I caught a glimpse of Potters Bar. The whole journey took two days and the filming of a match between de Vicenzo, Yancey and myself ran on into two more days. Roberto won, I was second, and Bert third, but it seemed crazy travelling so far to play 18 holes. We were on the plane again four days after leaving Palm Springs, and on our way to Phoenix, Arizona. It was the American tour again and despite a sixty-nine in the second round I missed the cut. But on that second day I hit the ball farther than I had ever done and this was the start of a wonderful run. We moved on to Doral in Florida and were joined there by my mother and father who were making their first visit to the U.S. I made the last day and felt that things were beginning to happen. Both Viv and I were completely at home in our new, ever-changing environment. She came back one day after a hair-do with what I thought was an astronomical bill, so I bought a small do-it-yourself book on hair-dressing, some scissors and clippers and started to cut her hair myself. She says that if ever we need to we will be able to open up a hair-dressing business at home with the boss of the outfit very much a working partner. It also helped having my parents with us—we used to go out to a different restaurant each night and over huge meals talk about the old days and all our friends, the Powells and Williamsons and the fellas at the steel works and the golf club.

I had felt for a few weeks that my game was beginning to change—I was using my legs more and at the next stop, Orlando, I finished fourth. My mother was astounded at the prize money and because she has a true Yorkshirewoman's appreciation of its value was absolutely thrilled when I won several thousand dollars by finishing second at Pensacola. I had hit form and had a great chance of winning but at the seventeenth hole the fourth time round I came down on a little wedge shot too quickly, and knocked the ball over the green to leave George Archer, who went on to win the Master the following year, in first place.

Looking back through my career I find that I have generally played well in bursts of a few weeks. I knew I was enjoying one at Pensacola, then at Jacksonville next week came my first victory in the U.S. There have been many turning points through the years, but this was perhaps the biggest of them. The swing had started to stay slow after my return from Nairobi and when it does that I always feel that I might be in business. At least for a while. I had been fourth, second and this victory introduced a new, little-known face to the newspapers and television screens on both sides of the Atlantic. The first prize of just over £8,000 was almost as much as I had earned from two victories in England and from all the other tournaments round the world the previous year.

After two rounds I was joint leader with Doug Sanders and after playing the third round with Arnold Palmer I was a shot in front. The third man with Palmer and me in the last two rounds was Don January, a marvellously relaxed, slow-moving Texan who, while appearing to sleep-walk most of the time, is, in fact, one hell of a player. When playing he peers out on life from under a floppy hat and I always feel that Don would as soon make for the nearest grass bank and have a sleep as continue the round.

I had now played with Palmer on several occasions and although his army can be a little troublesome I find him the perfect partner. It looked bad for me when he birdied the first hole to get level but I was soon ahead again and, almost unconscious of what was happening and certainly not daring to allow myself to think of victory, I finished in seventy-one to win by two shots. During that purple patch I shot nine consecutive rounds of seventy or under and I doubt if I will ever repeat such a run.

January and Palmer could not have been kinder and afterwards Palmer, who thinks so much of Britain and holds our golf courses in such high regard, sent a telegram to the British P.G.A. congratulating them on producing a U.S. tour winner.

I was hardly away from a Press or T.V. camera or microphone for a couple of days and I remember getting a call from the B.B.C. in the early hours of the following morning (I was still in bed when it came), and to this day I have no idea what I said. Friends tell me that I used the word 'super' a few million times. I hope those who heard that chat from between the sheets will forgive me. It was how I felt. Super!

With all that cash on its way to the bank I tried to be smart and took a week off to prepare for the Masters. Some friends flew out from England believing that the youngster the papers were calling 'Jacksonville Jacko' might become the first British winner at Augusta, but after a sixty-nine in the first round which kept me only a shot off the pace my golf got worse and worse and I finished out of the first twenty. There was a temporary return to form in the Tournament of Champions in which I finished seventh but I failed to make much show on either side of the Atlantic for the rest of the year. The Open was played at Carnoustie which I rate one of the world's toughest courses and after a few holes of the third round I was ahead but I took a confidence sapping eight after driving into a bunker at the eleventh and finished an embarrassingly long way behind Player who survived by two shots after a great battle with Nicklaus over the last few holes.

I was never going well until the last round of the British P.G.A. at Royal mid-Surrey and after going into the last round of the Dunlop Masters well clear I had one of the most desperate experiences of my life. Thomson, the winner and my partner, picked up shots on me at the first two holes and, in heavy rain, murdered me.

The year ended in Britain with defeat against Player in the semi-final of the Piccadilly Match-Play Championship. The match was an extraordinary one and in the last nine holes of a two-round match I had four birdies and an eagle to square with the South African on the last green where in appallingly murky conditions he missed from a couple of feet.

I had come back after appearing dead with nine to play and was disappointed when the umpire gave the old cricket ruling: 'Bad light stops play.' The rains continued all through Saturday, and washed out play, and we got up at dawn on Sunday morning for the extra holes. Wentworth was still very damp and after Player had holed from nine feet for a birdie four, I missed from only three feet to lose. It was a bitter disappointment, for the Piccadilly is now established as the Match-Play classic of the year.

I played in Australia in November and after Christmas at home, Viv and I began our journeyings again. Six months later we were back at Royal Lytham for the Open Championship.

My earnings from tournament winnings and other sources in 1968 were said to be in the region of £40,000 and I went to America this time with the feeling that I was accepted as an established tour player. Nothing that happened in the next few months gave me any indication that this was in fact going to be the greatest year of my life.

After another unsuccessful bid for the Masters I became very disheartened and a fortnight later asked Vivien to ring the airline and book us a flight home. I had failed to make the cut again and was completely fed up with tour life and all that was going with it. I had been working on better leg action after studying the style of a number of players—Tommy Bolt, Nicklaus, Palmer, Yancey and Weiskopf in particular. The traditional method of teaching and playing in Britain is based on hitting against a firm, locked left side. But after studying the people I have mentioned and film of a number of other players,

I realised that the Americans had moved way beyond the old fashioned method which I had been taught. To get maximum power one must slide the hips through to the ball with the knees moving through at the same time. I was working on this new action which requires both perfect timing and great strength in the legs during that sad spell early in 1969 but for so long I could not get everything going at the same time.

During our retreat from the scene of disappointment I told Viv that even though I could not have stayed there any longer, missing cuts and getting into a thoroughly bad frame of mind, we must get back soon. At home I played a few rounds with friends, found the new leg action working better and began to feel better again about my putting. After a break of only ten days I returned to Kemper, played in the Western Open and then showed up well with rounds of seventy-one and seventy in the U.S. Open at Houston. Orville Moody won there after only eighteen months on the tour and any chance I had of troubling the leaders disappeared with a bad start in the third round and a seven on the ninth hole.

I had been thinking a lot about leg action and getting the tempo slow again and although my form so far during the year was not that of a man about to win the Open Championship, when we came back to England I felt happier with my game than I had been for a long time.

I have, I think, learned to pace myself properly. A year earlier at Carnoustie I had been in a good position after two rounds but was beginning to run out of steam. It is a strange sensation. I feel I do not want to have anything to do with golf, let alone play in big money tournaments; and I cannot play well unless I really have that desire thing which I find myself talking about so often. I often feel that people watching can tell when I am in the right mood with all the desire going for me. They must be able to see at other times how bored I am looking. I must have looked that way an awful lot in the months preceding the 1969 Open.

There must be a limit to the frequency with which one can bring out this great hungry desire and all I know is that I play much better when I am completely rested. In America, before returning for the Open, I knew for the first time exactly what I was working on and felt that this change which had taken so long to come into effect would soon reap rewards. Looking back I feel that the bad times of the earlier months were due to my falling between two stools of the game, the one I had been taught and the method I knew I must adopt.

VI

The British Open Championship
Royal Lytham and St. Annes, 1969

VI

The British Open Championship
Royal Lytham and St. Annes, 1969

The final putt, the last of the 120 I made during four days of numbed suspense and occasional ecstasy at Royal Lytham and St. Annes, a pleasantly short one of around half an inch, disappeared from view and seconds later I was throwing the ball high into the stands. A Briton was again Open champion of his country and I was that Briton.

Viv ran across and said, 'Well done, darling.' She needed to say nothing. The tears told of her joy and final relief that the Open Championship of 1969 was all over. Mum and Dad, dozens of friends from Lincolnshire and Potters Bar, and what seemed like the whole of Britain seemed to feel the same way.

Almost the first fellow I spoke to was Nicklaus. I said, 'God, Jack, I never knew anyone could be so scared, so frightened.' He grabbed me warmly and said, 'Don't worry. It happens to everyone in the big ones. They say it even happened to Hogan.'

I have been asked many times what I felt most at the time. I think most of all there was this feeling that I had won something every golfer in the world wants to win. It was a feeling I will keep all my life. This was an experience no one can ever take away, not when others win the trophy, nor even if someone sneaks into our house near Brigg and steals the replica. I knew that July afternoon at Royal Lytham and St. Annes that I would always have this moment to look back on and the memory of it will never die.

All that I had worked for had come true over a spell of four days and 280 shots. There might be another year, another major victory, other great occasions. Somehow I was all alone there, isolated from the tens of thousands of people. Wonderful things will happen to others. But this was my Everest, and no one can ever take away the recollection of that moment when I sat on its peak.

As far as my game was concerned, I knew after that final seventy-two which enabled me to hold off Bob Charles by two shots with Peter Thomson and Roberto de Vicenzo another stroke behind that it could stand up to the fiercest pressure. I knew that I could keep the tempo slow and the swing right under the greatest stress. Until then I had never been sure.

I had won tournaments before, winning a great deal more than the Open prize of £4,250 when I collected just over £8,000 at Jacksonville the year before, but the strain was in no way comparable. For this was the British Open, a title fought for first by the best players in Scotland, then of Britain and for fifty years one of the major targets of the best players in the world.

I had lived most of that wonderful day in a mental vacuum. The night before, when I held a two shot lead, I had quite a big dinner at the house Viv and I shared with the Yanceys but knew that sleep was out of the question without some help. Viv must have sensed this and gave me a sleeping tablet. Before the end of the midnight movie on television I was snoring my head off and Yancey gave me a fireman's lift up to bed and dumped me in beside Vivien.

The moment I woke I knew there was no escape. Maybe there would be a downpour and play would be put off? But it was a fine bright Lancashire morning. I had a steak and a couple of fried eggs, looked at the papers to assure myself that I really was leading in what many were saying was the hottest Open field of all time.

My Dad came round to the house. He did not say much, just wandered about, nibbling at a bit of toast, sipping coffee. I knew why he was there and he knew. He just wanted to be with me. He talked a little more as time dragged by, but nothing any of us said meant much. We all knew what victory would mean but none of us dared think about it.

I kept saying to myself that never for one moment in the next few hours must I let my thoughts stray to the rewards which were likely to come to me if the name Jacklin was still up there in front on the leaderboard at the end of the afternoon. We went up to the course where the early starters were already playing and I changed slowly for a short spell on the practice ground.

Throughout the week of the championship I had hit a few practise shots with nine and eight irons and then done the bulk of my work with a seven iron. I was now beginning to feel that the slow tempo and use of my legs were becoming a natural part of my swing, and as these were the things I had worked on so the past few weeks, I felt some kind of new confidence.

There seemed no point in going through all the clubs in the bag while practising. I figured that it was easier to get the rhythm by concentrating on one club, and on that Saturday it was a bit late to do anything but get warmed up. By the time

Bob Charles and I came under starters orders I was in some sort of state of limbo, not really there, but at the back of my mind fully aware of what I had to do and of what victory would bring. But these things had to be kept way back, in some sort of little pocket not to be opened until the best, or worst had happened.

My plan for playing a good test of golf, but not, in my view, a great course, had been worked out during the previous ten days. My preparation during that time had been what racing people call a light one, half an hour or so's work-out and only one practice round. Each day I played most of the time with Bert Yancey and he often wanted to have another nine holes in the afternoon but I preferred to go back to bed and think through what had happened in the round we had just played.

So I set off for the most momentous round of my life so far, with a two shot lead over Christy O'Connor and Charles. I was on 208 and just a stroke behind those in joint second place were five times winner Peter Thomson and Hoylake hero de Vicenzo. Brian Huggett and Nicklaus, who had short a third round sixty-eight, were on 213.

In my battle plan for the week I was content to carry the traps in front of the short first with a five iron allowing the ball to run up to the green. I had a two there with a six yard putt in my first hole of the championship but was perfectly happy with the threes I made there in rounds two and three. I made three there to begin the final struggle satisfactorily . . . it is always enough to get away to a par start.

The wind had been behind all week on the opening holes and it was impossible to stop the ball on the greens with the longer irons. With a one iron off the tee at the second I was down the middle and a five iron and two putts gave me my par there . . . the fourth four I had made at this hole.

At the third, where I again used a one iron from the tee, I hit a four iron second to sixteen feet and holed the putt for a birdie. Bob took four and I was three ahead. My caddy, who had taken his own sleeping mixture, a bottle of scotch, the night before, said nothing as we went up the fourth fairway after a good shot with the driver and I remember saying to him, 'For God's sake, say something. Not necessarily about golf or what's happening. Just say something.' He chatted about mostly nothing for the rest of the afternoon.

I had another good break at the fourth, a shortish par four where I had previously taken three-four-five. Golf is, in the final analysis, all about figures and it is understandable that they often run through one's head and I found myself thinking that if I kept up this sequence and took six I might be sunk. But I hit a seven iron forty feet from the flag and holed a tram-liner of a putt for a three. I remember catching Viv's eye in the crowd and apparently I gave her an enormous wink.

There are players like Palmer who like to make a charge from behind but I like to lead. But the great fear of the front runner is that over the opening holes in the last round things will go wrong and the lead slip away. The reverse had now happened and I was five shots ahead. Maybe the Open was going to be mine, but, hell, I must not think about it. The next hole and then the next and so on must be the only things in my mind.

I had played a six iron at the short fifth in the first two rounds and made a two and a three. Now I took a five, overshot the green, and took four and the gap between the quiet, poker-faced

New Zealander and myself was only four. Bob is not the easiest of fellows to play with because only rarely does he register the slightest emotion, but he is a really genuine and likeable type.

The sixth gave me trouble all week, and my misfortunes there all stemmed from one drive during practice. This tee shot flew over the traps on the left-hand side of the fairway and stupidly I got it into my head that I could in fact carry these traps. I tried to do so each time and twice caught the rough near them with what might have been disastrous results. This time my tee shot finished close to a small tree in very deep grass and I had to sit astride the tree and thump a sand iron out on to the fairway. A seven iron took me to the green which Bob had reached in two and for a moment I could see us being back to where we were at the start of the round.

Bob was too strong with his first putt and I got down in two for my par. He missed his return putt so the situation mercifully remained unchanged. We both made quite remarkable fours at the 553 yard seventh where you must hit a perfectly accurate and long tee shot. Bob's second was badly off line and he was left with a third from long grass to a pin placed only fifteen feet beyond a greenside bunker. He floated a sand iron just past the lip of the bunker and finished only three feet from the hole. Certainly one of the greatest shots I have ever seen—but one I must not let shake me!

I was trapped on the left but came up well to seven feet and holed the putt for a matching birdie four. The next, a comparatively easy four with a second shot onto a plateau green, brought us both fours and we then had par threes at the short ninth. In the third round here I holed from thirty-four feet for a two but now I just missed from twelve feet to take three. Bob had an escape at this one where he almost shanked his tee shot, but he chipped quite close and made his par.

The tenth, where the only danger is to the right, is a hole at which you look for a birdie but I failed to make one there all week. Charles played a beautiful approach to within eight feet and holed the putt. The huge crowds grew all the time as people doubled back from the matches in front and news came with them that O'Connor was not likely to fight it out with Bob and me.

Thomson and de Vicenzo were not making any great impression either and in fact the only player on this last day to tear the course apart was Peter Alliss who had a sensational five under par sixty-six to shoot through the field and finish on 286.

Only four others bettered par all day, Kel Nagle, Miller Barber, Neil Coles and Cobie Le Grange.

Now three shots ahead with eight to go I played the eleventh exactly as planned, driving over the bunkers, hitting a one iron low along the right hand side of the fairway and wedging to the green. All the trouble—and it is pretty frightening stuff at that—is on the left hand side, and there was simply no point in attempting a very big second to the green.

I wedged to twenty-five feet and hit the hole with my putt and then at the most difficult short hole on the course, the twelfth, cashed in on the sort of bunker shots which had saved me three times in the last four holes on the previous day.

My tee shot found a trap on the right hand side but I came out to within four feet and holed to maintain my advantage. Things now looked fairly bright. I had set off on this perilous journey two shots to the good and now with two thirds of it covered had increased my advantage to three. There was a hold

up on the thirteenth tee when the binding on Bob's driver came
unwound. He tried to repair it himself and was about to send
his caddy back to the clubhouse for another driver when I offered
to do the repair. My mind went back to the hours I had spent in
Bill Shankland's shop at Potters Bar and I fixed the binding so
that we could carry straight on. The one thing I did not want at
that time was a long delay—and maybe Bob would be impressed
by my coolness.

My second here was perhaps the unluckiest shot I played all
week. It looked a perfect wedge but the ball bounced on into
the long grass which is a hazard round the greens on many good
championship courses.

Charles was safely on in two and got his par four. All I could
do was hack the ball out short and two putts to get down meant
that we were level on the round.

The fourteenth needed an accurate drive slightly left because
out right there is a mound and all sorts of trouble. I gave my tee
shot everything. That precious lead over Charles, for it was now
clear that the Open Championship of 1969 was a battle between
the two of us, must not be allowed to slip any further.

Bob came off his second and finished after a bad kick short
on the left and in a bunker. I almost made three, settled happily
for a four and with my opponent struggling to a five the gap
opened to three again.

I had a great chance at the fifteenth to go further ahead where
Charles had pulled his second near the ropes but I made a poor
first putt from a few yards in front of the green which left the
ball eight feet short. I missed, he got his five and I was still three
up. I had had threes in the second and third round at the easy
sixteenth but this time had to settle for a four when my first putt

rolled over the hole. Bob got his par and I knew then that I was a virtual certainty to win.

We both hit good drives at the seventeenth where it is essential to go out to the right and he hit a super second which perhaps a little unluckily stayed right to finish pin high just off the green.

Going up the fairway friends who had lived through it all with me during the afternoon shouted their encouragement and both Bob and I knew that the Open Championship lay between us. I was a little short with my second and again short with my first putt from twenty yards. Bob chipped very close to the hole but I still had a good chance of making four. I turned the blade of my putter just a fraction and missed on the left hand side, took five, but was still two ahead with one to play. Exactly how I felt in the next few minutes remains something of a blur.

There was a terrific reception for both of us on the tee and Bob slightly pushed his drive. Someone shouted that he was in the bunker but I asked Willie and he confirmed what I thought —that the ball had just cleared the trap.

Home was only a few hundred yards and less than ten minutes away, a haven with a wonderful welcome after four days of tremendous tension and swinging fortune.

I stepped up to the ball and said to myself, 'Go to it. This is it.' I knew then, as I had known all through that long afternoon, that with just this last hurdle to cross that not a thing must enter my head. No thoughts of the fame, the fortune. I had this final drive to hit and as I had been hitting super drives all day apart from the one at the sixth, it never crossed my mind to play safe and hit a two or three iron or maybe a three wood. Had

I geared down in this way some seed of doubt might have come niggling into my mind and ruined my concentration.

Sixes at the last hole at Lytham have cost a number of people previous championships, Scot Eric Brown and Irishman Christy O'Connor among them, and a pulled tee shot had cost Nicklaus a five here in 1963 when a four would have put him level with Charles and Rogers. I had had a slight tendency all week to hook a little from the tee and I decided to drive down to the right of those bunkers where disaster had struck so often in the past and fade the ball off them into the fairway.

I stood over the ball, hit exactly the shot I wanted, and heard the tremendous cheering of the vast crowds ahead as my ball bounced merrily into the centre of what had become my victory highway.

From the tee there was still 389 yards to go of the 27,392 yards journey which had begun so happily on the Wednesday with a birdie two on the first hole. Willie and I chatted for a moment and I walked happily to my ball which was in a position to give me the perfect set-up for the four which I knew must make me the first Briton to win the title in eighteen years. Charles hit a perfect second right of the flag and as he is undoubtedly one of the finest putters golf has ever known I knew that he was in a position to make three. I had hit that drive far enough to make the green comfortably with an eight iron but all week I had been hitting seven irons well in practice and I felt sure that for this vital shot, a controlled half seven, was the one for me. I had a practise swing, looked ahead for a moment at the target and as the crowd raced in from both sides of the fairway just got a glimpse of that beautiful little white ball nestling only four yards right of the hole. There was surely no way that I could take more than two from there so Charles could still get his birdie and I would be Open Champion. But for an earthquake or a heart attack—and my heart, although pounding a bit, was in good shape—I knew that the Championship was mine.

We battled through the milling, happy crowd ahead. I lost a shoe when someone trod on my heel, picked it up and when I got through the jostling thousands with a couple of huge policemen helping me. I slipped my foot into the shoe although the lace remained untied until later.

The reception as I made my way over the last hundred yards or so was fantastic. I knew that somewhere there ahead of me were my Mum and Dad who had done so much to launch this dream and make it come true, Viv who, over the last three years, had shared the occasional triumph and borne with me in those times of disappointment, and I wanted to be with them all.

But even then it crossed my mind that something daft might happen. How the hell anyway was I going to keep my hand steady enough to make those last putts. Or maybe one putt. I might drop the putter on the ball and incur a penalty. Or touch it as I addressed it. It was amazing the things that went through my mind with the goal of a lifetime only a few seconds away.

A lot of the older British pro's—I remember Dai Rees particularly—were up there in the stands and in all the din I heard Dai shout, 'Good old Tony.'

Safely on to the green with people cheering from the windows and the balcony of the clubhouse, I remember saying to myself that you don't win an Open Championship with a shoelace undone and somehow in the middle of it all I kept my hands steady enough to tie it up.

Charles hit a super putt but it did not break in from the right as he expected and stayed out. My own line from four yards was I thought the same but the ball stayed just a little right and fractionally short of the hole. From half an inch I had three to win. The show was being transmitted by T.V. satellite to many parts of the world, as well as being watched in millions of homes in Britain, and, as I walked forward I could hear the cameras whirring above the strange silence of the crowd.

I tapped the ball in and the Open Championship was mine.

I have told of my immediate reactions, of my feelings about that moment which will be with me for ever. There were television interviews, talks to my friends of the British Press—men like Henry Longhurst, Ron Heager, Bob Rodney, Keith Mackie, Ben Wright, Pat Ward-Thomas, Leonard Crawley, Peter Ryde, Peter Dobereiner, Tom Scott, John Ingham, Mark Wilson and Maurice Hart who in the few years I had been on the circuit had done so much to help and encourage me.

George Simms, the Press Officer who for the previous three days had guided me through conferences after the rounds of 68-70-70 which had taken me to that precious last day lead, steered me through the crowds and I sank a bottle of lager in one. Before talking, though, of the immediate results of victory on that great Lancashire stage, I should refer to the earlier rounds, in each of which I putted better than on the last day, having eight single putts in round one, six in round two and seven on the Friday against only four singletons in my final seventy-two.

In the first round Charles had broken the record with a sixty-six and Hedley Muscroft, a Yorkshireman capable of brilliant performances, was with me on sixty-eight, while Jack Nicklaus appeared on that first day to ruin what many considered before the Championship to be a favourite's chance with a seventy-five. Of the others who finished in the first ten, Thomson and O'Connor had seventy-ones, de Vicenzo seventy-two, Davis Love, an American little known outside the U.S.A., seventy, Alliss, seventy-three, and Nagle seventy-four. An American with high hopes after that first round was the extraordinary Miller Barber who began with a sixty-nine. The man known as Mr. 'X' on the U.S. tour then had two seventy-fives before finishing with another sixty-nine. I began in a way beyond my wildest hopes holing a six yarder for a two at the first, a ten footer for a three at the fourth, a twenty footer for a two at the fifth and a five yarder for a four at the sixth, putting me four under par after only six holes. If I failed to keep up the fireworks—I had a four at the short ninth and a five at the par four fourteenth—my sixty-eight was enough to give me the sort of start that makes any title-hunter happy. In the second round I was in trouble at the sixth when I drove into the rough, hit a three wood into a bank, moving the ball only about twenty yards, but finally got away with a par five when I holed from ten yards. Towards the end of the third round I hit some bad shots and only with what seemed at the time and still seems to this day to be incredible bunker play did I maintain the pressure and lead with one round to go. There was one giant putt of eleven yards at the ninth for a two, and at the eighth, fifteenth, seventeenth and eighteenth I came out of bunkers and got down with a single putt. I had not worked particularly hard on sand trap play before the Championship but if the mastery of any one shot won me the title, it was this ability to get up and down, as they say, in two.

My recovery from sand at the eighth finished only two feet from the hole and I was a foot nearer from the trap at the fifteenth. I came out to two feet at the seventeenth and then at the last from the bunker right of the green to only four feet.

Most of the year I had been in a black mood over my putting but in the Championship which was to bring so many changes into my life, I had twenty-five single putts and went to the seventy-first hole before I three putted. In a golfing sense, as I said earlier, victory under great pressure gave me the belief that I would be able to again produce my best golf when the tension mounts and the heat is on.

What of the material rewards which follow a victory of this sort. My manager, Mark McCormack, made the claim that so long as I continue to play well and keep my name going, victory at Lytham might mean a total of a million dollars as a direct reward over the coming years.

All of this, as he pointed out, because I had won a title which had been in the hands of invaders since 1952.

I did not appreciate just what Mark meant by this claim. I was, in any case, too mixed up in other things for Jack Rubins of Potters Bar gave me a wonderful party and the celebration went on long into the night.

McCormack delayed a trip to South Africa for a few days in order to set in motion the merchandising which will assure me of a very handsome income for the next five years. A British Open Champion, and a young reasonably presentable one at that was a gift from the gods for the man who made huge fortunes for his first client Arnold Palmer and then for Gary Player and Jack Nicklaus.

The week after Lytham I went down to Royal St. Georges at Sandwich to play in the Piccadilly Knock-out Tournament. The sponsors gave me a suite overlooking the sea in the Guildford Hotel and before I had been there two days I realised what Mark meant when he talked about a million dollars. My phone hardly stopped ringing. It seemed that every manufacturer in the country wanted me to wear, use, drive or drink his products.

One chap wanted to clothe me throughout, and the range of inquiries staggered me. Over the next few months many of these deals were sorted out and I hope I do not sound too commercial when I say that winning for Britain at Royal Lytham in 1969 also meant winning for Jacklin on a scale which still to me seems unbelievable.

I have signed a contract to wear sweaters, shirts and slacks for a leading manufacturer, and the McCormack organisation negotiated for me a contract with the Dunlop Sports Company. There have been deals with a shoe concern, a whisky firm, an airline and a number of other organisations.

Newspaper articles and an instructional strip have been done. I have played a number of exhibition matches at a very rewarding fee and taken part in games for television. One of these took place the week after our son, Bradley, was born and I was delighted on all counts that he arrived exactly on time in December 1969. I had told I.T.V. and Esso that I would not leave Viv, to play in their tournament at Great Lucaya Beach unless Bradley made the tee-off time the doctors had given him and when he did so I caught a plane a couple of days later for the Caribbean. The field was quite strong, including Nicklaus and Player, and because Master Bradley Mark Jacklin arrived on schedule, the family bank account was boosted by £6,000.

The year of victory at Lytham was a memorable and an incredible one. Only five years before I had come back from a frustrating tour of South Africa owing £400 and with only £130 in the bank. My maths have improved since then but at the time I remember working out that I was £270 on the wrong side.

Later in 1969 we entertained the Americans in the Ryder Cup at Royal Birkdale and I was fortunate to go through all six matches without being beaten. But more of that later. Viv and I moved into our new house at Elsham, near Brigg, and not too far from Scunthorpe where I was born.

I bought the place, a lodge on the Elwes Estate, for a little over £10,000 and as I had had a good year in 1968 with tournament and other earnings of around £40,000, Viv and I decided to make it the sort of home in which we can live for the rest of our lives. I got a builder chum of mine to start on elaborate structural alterations—another £10,000 worth—but after starting 1969 rather poorly I had got cold feet about all the outgoing cash.

In fact, the Jacklin home looked for a while as if it would not be quite the place it now is. But on the night of victory at Lytham, I made a phone call to my builder friend. I told him to go ahead and to hell with the expense.

In Bradley's nursery one wall depicts a golfing scene with the players a string of nursery rhyme characters and the little fellow at the end of the sequence is holding a putter and knocking the ball in from a couple of feet. I have no idea whether Bradley will follow me into golf, but if he does I will do everything I can to encourage him.

The year ended with a letter from the Royal Chamberlain telling me that I had been awarded the O.B.E. I immediately thought of many other people in sport who perhaps deserve this honour before me. One who came to mind was jockey Lester Piggott, but I was thrilled to learn of this honour when still only twenty-five.

I had to keep the secret until the New Year. It was terribly difficult, but I did so, and did my best to sound surprised when early in January some press friends rang to tell me that I would soon be on my way to Buckingham Palace.

VII

Playing for Great Britain in two Ryder Cups

VII

Playing for Great Britain in two Ryder Cups

The mood of the British team which went to Houston for the Ryder Cup match of 1967 was one of defiant optimism. Non-playing captain Dai Rees did a great job in making us believe in ourselves against all the odds and when the matches finished the American skipper Ben Hogan said of the side beaten 23½–8½. 'This is one of the finest teams you have ever put out against us.'

Why, if this was true, did we lose by such a wide margin? It was, I am afraid, the old story of our matching Hogan's men for long periods of almost every match and then failing over the last few holes. We were certainly not out-hit over the 7,166 yard heavily wooded course with its never ending series of water hazards; but we failed too often to get down in two from off the green while the Americans did so.

There was much talk at the time that this might be the last of the series. Britain had to look back to 1957 for her last victory, the big American T.V. companies did not consider the Houston match worth screening, and there was the suggestion that biennial matches between the might of U.S. golf and the rest of the world would be a more attractive proposition for all concerned.

We stayed in Houston, were taken to the space centre, and

One of those rare moments of leisure. Tony, away from it all, goes out shooting. (C.S.)

At home, in his new house at Elsham. (C.S.)

Two fine photographs, emphasising Jacklin's great technique; the first on the practice ground, the second, in competitive anger. (F.G. both)

At Royal St. George's, Sandwich, scene of the Dunlop Masters, 1967.
Jacklin receives the winner's cheque after his first major tournament win, having broken the course record with a sixty-four in the final round, which included a hole-in-one at the short sixteenth. (F.G.)

British Open, 1969.
Superb driving and bunker play underpinned Tony's victory.
Here he demonstrates both (F.G. both).

Jacklin acknowledges the crowd, having holed out on the eighteenth green. A home player is British Open champion at last. (F.G.)

British Open, 1969.

Later, with Vivienne and the trophy. (F.G.)

British Open, 1969.
Tony 'conducts' the gallery, as they spontaneously break into 'For he's a
jolly good fellow' at the victory ceremony. (F.G.)

Agony and relief. Tony unmasks all the pressures of the tournament trial as a putt slips by and a trap-shot goes close to the hole. (C.S. both)

treated with the wonderful hospitality to which visiting teams have become accustomed. Dai, aware of the criticisms and the threat to the continuation of the matches which apart from all else do the finances of our P.G.A. a power of good, whipped us into a mood of more than cautious optimism, and after he had finished with us there was the feeling that we had at least an outside chance. What an inspiring little man he is!

Huggett, blessed with the same brand of courage and fight, partnered George Will in the first foursome against Casper and Boros and they gave us a flying start by winning the first two holes. Casper and Boros hit back at the fourth and sixth to square it but a birdie at the eighth put us ahead again. We dropped shots at the thirteenth and fourteenth to go one down but birdied the fifteenth and with pars over the home stretch finished all square. Not a bad start for a bunch of no-hopers.

Palmer and Dickinson won the second hole with a birdie against Alliss and O'Connor but the pair generally regarded as our anchor men levelled things by the turn. The Americans won the next two, and when we looked to have a chance of getting one back at the thirteenth after Dickinson had driven into the trees Palmer produced one of those fighting recovery shots for which he is famed and made the green. Peter and Christy battled on but lost two and one.

I was terribly nervous before my first game for the British side but it helped to have big Dave Thomas around. The cheerful Welshman is an ideal partner . . . I knew that whatever happened we would not be out-hit when it was his tee-shot . . . and we reached the turn in thirty-five against Sanders and Brewer to be two up. We quickly went farther ahead against two men woefully below their best and won four and three. It was cer-

tainly a happy start to my international career after just making
the side by finishing tenth in the 1967 order of merit, with total
prize money of £3,393 and a stroke average in nine tournaments
of 71.44.

Coles, who had travelled by land and sea for the matches,
played with his close chum Hunt but they could never get into
it against Pott and Nichols and after turning three down
were beaten five and four. The score stood 2–1 in favour of the
U.S. with one match halved and not surprisingly Rees dropped
Hunt and Coles during the lunch break and brought in Gregson
and Hugh Boyle, who like me were new boys to the series.

Unhappily, they found Palmer and Dickinson, the man who
modelled himself on his skipper Hogan, in completely irresist-
ible form. The Americans hit the faltering newcomers with four
birdies in the outward nine and with a score of thirty-two
against a disappointing three over par thirty-nine were set for
a victory which came on the fourteenth green.

Will and Huggett again had a tremendous match against
Casper and Boros and both pairs were out in thirty-four and all
square. Although they dropped shots at the tenth and fifteenth
they were round in sixty-nine, losing by one hole on the last
green. Hogan replaced the out of form Sanders and Brewer
with Gene Littler and Al Geiberger, and Thomas and I were
level with the new pair after an outward thirty-seven.

Gene and Al hit a bad patch, enabling us to win the eleventh
and thirteenth in par and a par three at the short sixteenth gave
us a three and two win. Alliss and O'Connor were again narrow
losers, this time against the very obviously in-form Pott and
Nichols and the scoreline read U.S. five, Britain two, with one
match halved.

The beautiful Houston course wore a misty veil when we began the four ball matches and I thought of Wentworth and Sunningdale and Woodhall Spa in similar conditions with a haze hanging over the fairways and trees and the sun trying to sneak through. Early reports of the match between O'Connor and Alliss and Casper and Brewer shook me quickly out of my day-dream.

Against the pair generally rated our strongest the Americans birdied the third, fifth and ninth and were three up. They went on to birdie the twelfth and although Christy and Peter were round in par they were beaten three and two.

Pott and Nichols hit Coles and Hunt with a birdie at the sixth and an eagle three at the ninth. We won the tenth, lost the twelfth and thirteenth and the sub par golf continued, this time from the Britons who shot birdies at the fourteenth and fifteenth. The quiet men of the British side had matched the barrage of the Americans and Pott and Nichols were mighty relieved to get home by one hole.

Thomas and I had a wonderful match against Littler and Geiberger. After going out in thirty-three we were level but we went one up at the twelfth where neither Al or Gene could make par. Geiberger holed from twenty-five feet to get square, and we were one down to a birdie three at the fifteenth. Dave, keen to keep our unbeaten record, hit a super tee shot to the 180 yard sixteenth and holed the putt for a two but at the seventeenth I went out of bounds and Dave, after a short second and a miss from five feet, failed to get his par. A half at the last, and we were no longer unbeaten.

An unhappy morning for Britain ended with Sanders and Dickinson birdieing the fourteenth and fifteenth for a three and two win over Huggett and Will and this pre-lunch whitewash meant that we were trailing as the prophets said we would by 9–2 with one match halved.

Dave and I had another thrilling set-to with Geiberger and Littler, but our halved match was the best we could do all afternoon and with the sixteen singles left we were 12–2 down with two halved. By now even the ebullient Dai and conceded that we were heading for defeat but as we talked of the two days play over dinner we felt much better than a cold look at the scoreline might have entitled us to feel. There had been some terrific matches as Hogan was the first to point out.

My first taste of individual combat in the Cup matches was a little alarming. On the first hole Palmer sank a fifty foot putt and Arnold at his most imperious had me five down at the turn. I made a brief rally winning the twelfth where he went into the trees and the thirteenth and fourteenth to be only two down but drove into the trees at the fifteenth, which he birdied. We halved the next in four and I was a three and two loser.

I went down by the same margin in the afternoon to Dickinson, who putted tremendously and repeatedly won holes at which I thought I had a chance. Our victories with the cause already lost were by Huggett, who beat Boros one hole, Coles, who beat Sanders two and one and again two and one in the afternoon, and Alliss, victor by the same margin over Brewer.

Thomas halved with Littler, and Hunt fought a draw with Nichols to leave the final score at 23½–8½. There was again much talk on both sides of the Atlantic after the match that these one-sided encounters be stopped, but happily it was agreed that they should continue without Britain seeking reinforce-

ments from elsewhere and the Americans came to Royal Birkdale under Sam Snead in 1969.

Weeks before Snead and his team arrived in Southport it
became clear that Palmer had not done enough to qualify for
the side, and perhaps because of my own victory in the British
Open the critics gave us a chance in the build-up to the October
match. It made a pleasant change.

At the same time our non-playing captain, Eric Brown, was
exhaling his own mixture of fire and brimstone, revealing that
he had seen to it that the Birkdale fairways were narrowed and
the rough just off them really rough. I have always felt that
American players who are good enough to represent their country are quite able to hit the ball straight when the occasion
demands but Brown seemed delighted with his campaign to give
us a boost before battle began.

The Americans arrived on the Sunday and Huggett and I
were ordered to get to Southport that evening so that we could
meet our opponents. Elaborate arrangements were made to fly
us from Wales where Brian and I were playing in an exhibition,
but fog ruined the best laid plans of our skipper and we missed
the 'parade'.

The match was preceded by a series of social events—I think
it was Maurice Bembridge who said after his first taste of these
things that one had to be a scratch drinker to survive—and
when play began there was every reason to think that our side
with its sound mixture of experience and youth had a better
chance than for many years.

In the line-up we had the old stalwarts Coles, O'Connor,
Butler, Alliss, Huggett and Hunt and a flock of comparative
newcomers, Townsend, Bembridge, Gallacher, Caygill, Barnes

and myself. The skipper let me know on several occasions that he expected big things of an Open champion and I was really keen to go and delighted when he paired me with Peter Townsend in the foursomes.

We opened in the most heartening way possible with three birdies in a row against Dave Hill and Tommy Aaron and Peter clinched our three and one victory with one of the greatest shots of the week, a three wood to the green at the seventeenth. This set up our seventh birdie of the morning and we needed a par four at the unplayed eighteenth for a seven under par sixty-six. Townsend and I have a similar outlook and temperament and most people agree that we bring out the best in each other. I was delighted when he chipped very close at the last two holes to give us a second win of the day by one hole against Casper and Aaron.

Gallagher and Bembridge lost two of the first three to birdies against Trevino and Ken Still, but fought back to be square at the turn. The Scot then holed from four yards at the tenth and a birdie four at the seventeenth gave this second youthful pair victory by two and one.

With Coles and Huggett always on top against Barber and Floyd and the old firm of Alliss and O'Connor halving with Casper and Beard after drawing level with a birdie two at the fourteenth we stood three up at lunch on the first day with one halved.

Peter and I were the only winners in the afternoon but the margins by which the other pairs were beaten were narrow enough to keep our hopes high. Hill and Aaron squeezed home by one hole against Huggett and Coles. Butler and Hunt lost to Nicklaus and Sikes on the last green and Trevino and Littler beat Gallagher and Bembridge by two holes.

Going into the second day we were leading 4–3 with one halved, and the morning of the four-ball matches was another bright one for us. Brown made some changes and O'Connor and Townsend beat Hill and Douglas one up, Huggett and Caygill halved with Floyd and Barber. Our only loss came when Barnes and Alliss went down after a terrific struggle by one hole to Trevino and Littler.

I played with Coles, whose aggression I have always admired, and we certainly needed that sort of thing against Nicklaus and Sikes. We were two down after five, but finally went round with a better ball of sixty-five to win on the last green.

Our slender lead had been doubled to two, but after lunch the best we could do was for Neil and myself to halve with Trevino and Barber, with Bembridge and Hunt finishing the same way against Aaron and Floyd. With the sixteen singles left, the long-time underdogs of the competition were level.

O'Connor slaughtered Frank Beard five and four, a great achievement against the top money winner in the U.S. that year and Coles, Bembridge, and Butler all won. I was delighted to be drawn against Nicklaus, and even more delighted to take an unexpectedly early lunch having won four and three.

Jack and I had a great tussle in the afternoon. It was always close with the big fellow playing much better and holing more putts than he had done in the morning and I will always regard the forty-footer I holed on the seventeenth to square it as one of the most important of my life. He just missed his first putt on the eighteenth but got his four and then with a supreme gesture so typical of the man gave me my two-footer for a half, and a halved match which gave Britain a tie.

Just before this Huggett, having holed a six-footer to square with Casper on the eighteenth, broke down and wept thinking that this putt had won the match for Britain. Among other great performances on this memorable day was Gallagher's brilliant golf which put him four under par when beating Trevino at the fifteenth.

There were some explosive moments during the match be-tween Gallagher and Huggett and Still and Hill on the second day, the touch paper being lit when Huggett pointed out that the Americans had putted out of turn at the seventh hole. Hill and Still were booed by the crowds after more fireworks at the eighth and Hill said bitterly that he would never again play in this country.

But the end of a great week came with U.S. P.G.A. president Leo Fraser handing the trophy to Lord Derby, it having been decided that although it in fact still belonged to the U.S. each country should keep it for a year. May there be no need for such a gesture in 1971.

VIII

The British Tour

VIII

The British Tour

I left the British tour at the end of 1967 after winning the Pringle at Royal Lytham and the Dunlop Masters at Royal St. George's. I have never regretted the decision for I remain convinced that only in America where course construction and conditions favour attacking golf can young players develop their game and raise it to a point where they can win in the toughest international competition.

This is not being disloyal to my own country, but our courses were fashioned many years ago, and although great players like Peter Thomson have dismissed the game in the U.S. as little more than an exercise in target golf and big hitting, the facts prove him wrong.

Playing in Britain encourages a defensive attitude. The courses vary enormously from day to day and to attack the pin as players do in the U.S. is at best difficult and sometimes suicidal. Their wider fairways encourage everyone to hit out, thus putting a premium on length and the greens are usually big enough to encourage one to attack.

Bunkers should be placed in strategic positions but the harsh penalties inflicted by them on many of Britain's championship courses have no place in the U.S. My point is that bunkers should be fair at all times but those steep-sided horrors from which there is virtually no escape in one shot without playing out sideways or back down the fairway have long been outdated. There are thousands of them on our courses.

It is generally assumed that players make their own luck and that the good players are better able to take advantage of the breaks. But how can one write off as a stroke of misfortune an encounter with a trap which can cost as many as three shots? Fairway bunkers in the U.S. have sand of rough texture from which one can play a long iron, and those round the greens are filled with finer sand from which it is routine to splash out. I really feel that less is left to chance, and this must be a good thing for the development of one's game.

The watering of greens is at last becoming more popular in Britain but there has been widespread criticism of the practice on the lines that tossing the ball into the air on to a plum-pudding surface is not what golf is about. The pitch and run shot is not required so often when the greens are watered American fashion, but I have not noticed any gap in the armoury of the best Americans when they have to play this stroke.

Then there is the advantage to be gained in the long run of playing regularly under pressure. For much of the fifties and sixties our tournaments were dominated by a group of players headed by men like Dai Rees, Harry Weetman, Christy O'Connor, Max Faulkner and David Thomas. The atmosphere was often that of a genteel garden party and the players were content to make a comfortable living without too much travel and the inconvenience it brings.

The prize money was ridiculously low. For five years from

1962 Neil Coles was the top money winner and he earned little more than £25,000 over the period. The difference in playing for £20,000 instead of £2,000 is tremendous and it naturally breeds a tougher type of competitor. Because of the huge sums played for there is a constant stream of fine young golfers moving on to the U.S. circuit and results in the last few years have proved that there are as many as fifty players there capable of winning any big event.

Malcolm Gregson was the first of what I will call the new brigade of British golfers to break through. He won three times in 1967 and took the Harry Vardon Trophy since when Brian Huggett and Bernard Gallagher have won this greatly prized award. The public were clamouring for new faces and in recent years they have had them. But is the position of the tour in Britain any healthier?

The Alcan sponsors moved to Britain with their first tournament at St. Andrews in 1967. The total prize money was well over £50,000 but the events at the home of golf and then Royal Birkdale were both won by Gay Brewer and with many stars not in the line-up this Golfer of the Year jamboree did not fire the imagination of the public. It is not surprising that it has been decided to base the Alcan in the U.S. in future with one in four of their events coming to Britain against three in four during the first four-year cycle.

The promoters point out that many more people watched the Alcan in Portland, Oregon, than at either St. Andrews or Birkdale. The charge to spectators was two and a half times as much so it is obviously a very much better financial deal for them to stage it in America. The formula used to bring together the Golfer of the Year field is to hold a series of qualifying events on either side of the Atlantic but I am convinced places should have been reserved for the winners of the U.S. and British Opens, the Masters and U.S. P.G.A. In this way the public would have been assured of seeing the winners of world golf's Big Four events each season and this would assuredly have guaranteed the sort of take at the gate which would have kept the Alcan as primarily a British tour enterprise.

There was, as is admitted, a certain amount of bungling over the 1970 John Player Classic. When this tournament was announced the first prize of £25,000 was a world record which the sponsors believed would attract the majority of the top American and overseas players. Alas, Mr. Joe Dey, president of the U.S. Tournament Players Division, made it clear that his members would not be released as the Player Classic coincided with the Greater Hartford Open.

Rightly, in my view, Mr. Dey claimed that his members owed allegiance to a tournament which had been running for seventeen years and in spite of a series of appeals by the John Player organisers Mr. Dey refused to budge. Although I was allowed to play at Hollinwell, Nottingham, Dey told me that he felt strongly that any player who took the major part of his income from the U.S. tour should support the events on that tour. It was a difficult case to argue but because I am British the T.P.D. officials relented.

Nicklaus, one of the leaders of the 'rebels' who almost broke away from the U.S. P.G.A. two years ago, supports their view. He told me at St. Andrews, 'I am not playing at Hartford but I would consider myself a traitor if during the same week I played elsewhere solely because the prize money was higher.'

We find, then, that the sponsors of the two biggest events in the history of British golf are dissatisfied, the Alcan people with the crowds their costly promotion has attracted and the Player people because of the poor response to their appeals. Between them these two business giants contributed almost £140,000 of the 1970 prize total of £320,000 played and the position is a far from happy one.

The record crowds which flocked to Nicklaus's Open proved that there is support for top golf in this country. With more than 80,000 paying customers the 1970 Open was a smash hit but for one reason only . . . the fans knew that they were going to see a high proportion of the best players in the world. With so many other calls on their time and money the sports fans will only take the trouble to turn out if they know the cast is worthy of their effort.

There is growing support for multi-sponsored events and I believe the International Classic at Copt Heath, Birmingham, was a great success. Peter Butler, my team mate in the World Cup in Buenos Aires, had a lot to do with this Midlands event and it could well be that the future of professional golf in Britain lies in this sort of promotion.

The majority of tournaments in the U.S. are organised by Chambers of Commerce and the success of almost every tournament there is due to a city effort and not to that of one lone sponsor and one club.

Sponsors who have been in business as British tournament promoters for a number of years may have to combine so that dates become freed for multi-sponsors. I like the idea of various industries running their own events . . . a Motor Classic in the Midlands, Wool Classic in Yorkshire, Cotton Classic in Lancashire and so on. The interest in golf runs hotter now than it has ever done and it would be tragic if we slipped behind the rest of the world.

I would much prefer to live and play in Britain, but the opportunities are elsewhere. Peter Thomson is busily drumming up support for what he calls a world tour and there are surely enough players with no ambitions to play on the American circuit to guarantee the success of Peter's venture. The tour he suggests would take in Australia, the Far East, Europe and Britain and he produces figures to prove that the growth of the tours in his home country and the Far East is far greater than it is here.

In Spain and Italy prize money has doubled over the last couple of years and the Lancome perfume people intend branching out from Paris, the site of their first eight-man fifty-four-hole tournament, into other major European cities.

I have played only occasionally on the home tour in the last two years but remember being shocked at the small crowds which attended the majority of the tournaments. And the lack of enthusiasm of the television companies, both B.B.C. and I.T.V., in the run of the mill events reflected the general apathy. With cricket crowds growing smaller golf has a wonderful chance of moving in as the major summer attraction and if prize money were higher it might be possible to run a 'season' of bigger tournaments. But the timing must be right so that on the dates chosen an international field can assemble without any clashing with players' commitments in other parts of the world.

I feel that both Alcan and Players have failed us, the one by the stubborn retention of their qualifying system and the other by not ensuring that the date chosen for their first and therefore most important tournament was clear. The pity of it all is that British golf is the sufferer.

The attitude of some clubs is still Victorian. There are still many in which those terribly uncouth fellows the professionals are not allowed and others with fine courses who would rather barricade their sanctuaries than allow pros to play and the general public in to watch.

Much has been done to encourage young players but more must be done. In America the rookie must pass playing and other tests, and the provision of a P.G.A. school where youngsters can be vetted before being let loose on the tour world, would, I am sure, benefit the game. I recall wanting to go to South Africa in 1962 and being told in no uncertain terms by Bill Shankland that I was not yet ready. Many professionals would do their assistants a favour by keeping them to the grind of learning the game a little longer. The gaining of experience is an essential part of one's development but exposure too early to regular tournament play can be harmful.

My early years in tournaments were great fun, charging round with Caygill in a series of cars of doubtful vintage and erratic performance, staying in digs, eating fish and chips with an occasional steak supper treat. The income was in the region of £1,000 a year and there was little left when expenses had been met.

I remember once writing to mother and father to tell them that I had touched Dai Rees's driver, picked up a divot for Peter Alliss, actually talked to Harry Weetman. I was very much the rookie in a world dominated by the few at the top.

Of these I had most admiration as a player for O'Connor, the rugged, amusing Irishman whose natural talent for the game and facility to make golf look simple match that of Casper. Perhaps in these two the old country and California have produced the two easiest swingers of their time, men who hit the ball with the minimum of effort and fuss but to maximum effect. They call him 'Wristy Christy' for his hitting action is very much of a wrist flick. He is a wonderful character, a man of moods who enjoys the famous black beverage of Dublin, and his record in Britain is extraordinary. He has been in the first six in seven British Opens and many feel that had he been born later and been encouraged to go to the 'finishing school' in America he would, as he deserves, now be recognised as a world class player.

After Himself, as Christy is known, in Ireland, Neil Coles has proved himself the most consistent of our players. Neil has a shut face at the top of his back swing and hits through the ball with a long right arm. In this he was, among British players, several years ahead of his time. He has seldom done well in the Open until 1970 where he finished joint sixth and usually finds his form late in the season. But today Europe offers big prizes to be won earlier in the year and in 1970 he had won £10,000 up to the Open. He refuses to fly following an unhappy experience on a domestic flight some years ago and this has meant that he has played little in the U.S.; sad, because he has the game to do well there. But he is quite content with the good living he has carved for himself. (Talking of carving, he shares my love of carpentry but is much better at it, having made himself a boat and most of the furniture for his Surrey home.)

Dai Rees is a wonderful little man, and without ever winning he has had a remarkable record in the Open. Twelfth as long

ago as 1939, he was fourth in 1950, joint second in 1953 and
1944 and was beaten by only a shot by Palmer at Birkdale in
1961. He won the first of his four match-play championships
in 1936 but is proudest of all of his team's effort when winning
the Ryder Cup at Lindrick in 1957. Dai is a complete pro and a
source of much inspiration to young players. His great buddy
Max Faulkner has been around almost as long. Max has a spare
room full of putters, wardrobes packed with clothes which
make Doug Sanders look a conservative dresser, and he has
always been one of the most beautiful long iron players in the
world. His other love is fishing, and as a kid I spent hours
listening to his stories and still do when I get the chance. Now
in his fifties his zest matches that of the remarkable Rees and
through the years he has added much needed colour to the
British tour.

Alliss will be remembered as the great enigma. An American
pro is reported to have said of the handsome Peter, 'With your
looks and swing Fort Knox won't be big enough to hold the
loot!' This observation was never put to the test for Peter has
seldom played in the U.S. except in Ryder Cup matches in
which his record is second only to that of Eric Brown.

Alliss is now at Moor Allerton, Leeds, and it is said to be the
most modern club in Britain. There is even a telephone at the
eighteenth tee from which players can order their drinks and
go straight in to them. Peter is a fine after dinner speaker, lively
writer and brilliant T.V. commentator. Without hitting a golf
ball he will always have plenty going for him. I remember that
when I first started playing among the big boys he was one of
the first to ask me to play in practice with him. Invitations like
that were not all too frequent. He never really gave the American

tour a trial for, as he told me once, 'To do so would mean selling up here and staying there for three or four years. You must live the life of an American, do well there. There is no good going there and thinking of yourself as an outsider and to beat them, you have to join them.' It was sound advice which I remembered in 1968 and no-one was kinder when I eventually beat 'em.

His close friend, Dave Thomas, is another who has never quite capitalised on a fantastic long game. Dave tied with Thomson for the Open in 1958, losing the play-off, but he has always had a 'hang-up' when chipping and there seems to be no cure for his particular trouble. He has apparently tried them all.

Eric Brown was always a tremendous match player and although always ready to speak his mind he is not nearly as fiery as legend suggests. Harry Weetman lived with the tough power-man tag but was in fact one of the most delicately accurate short game players and finest putters on the tour. His wife, Freda, was always around with advice and support and it could be that Weetman had a manager long before a man called McCormack came on the scene.

Brian Huggett won the Vardon Trophy in 1968 and will always do well because he has great spirit and an enviable capacity for hard work. A gay little man, Brian, who showed just what courage he has when he holed a six-footer in the last-but-one match in the 1969 Ryder Cup at Birkdale.

There are many other great characters among the seasoned players, men like the Count Ken Bousfield, the gypsy, Eric Lester, Hugh (Noddy) Lewis and Yorkshiremen Hedley Muscroft, Lionel Platts and Alex Caygill and in his quiet way John

Panton who has been one of the mainstays of the game in Britain and one of its most popular characters.

I have not seen too much of the younger players except Peter Townsend, a regular competitor on the U.S. tour. We played together in the Ryder Cup at Birkdale and he had a terrific season in 1968 when he finished second to Gay Brewer in the Alcan and won the P.G.A. championship at Royal mid-Surrey. Since then Peter has had a rough time but he is determined to make the grade in the U.S. after a year of terrible putting troubles.

Brian Barnes might be anything when he shelves the unfortunate habit of having one bad round in a tournament and, although Bernard Gallagher has done little since, he must have played extremely well to become the youngest-ever holder of the Vardon Trophy.

Oosterhius is, as I said earlier when talking of the British Open, a wonderful prospect and Maurice Bembridge has been asked by Trevino to play an extended season in the U.S. Recently our young players have spent their winters abroad and with a number of them playing in the U.S. the future must be brighter as far as the Ryder Cup and future Open championships are concerned. I hope the enthusiasm of the new brigade is rewarded by the continued prosperity of the tour in Britain.

IX

The Great Players of My Day

IX

The Great Players of My Day

Three players have passed the million dollar mark in prize money. This is not to say they are greater than Hagen, Jones, Nelson, Hogan and Snead but because they have been the leaders in my time, the pace setters of modern golf, I must begin with Palmer, Casper and Nicklaus who achieved their personal six-figure hauls in that order.

Comparison of the stars of different eras makes for fascinating discussion but no firm conclusions are ever reached. Was Clay better than Marciano, either of them as good as Louis? And was the Brown Bomber in the same class as Jack Johnson? Is Jackie Stewart superior to Moss and Hawthorn, and did either of these stars of the fifties rate with Fangio? Is Sobers a finer cricketer than Miller, Compton, Hutton and Hobbs? How would Moore and Best rank with Matthews, Finney and James, We will never know the answers.

What is unquestioned is that Palmer was for a decade and more the greatest of his time. If he could putt these days, he might still be out in front. I have come to know him well and what is certain is that no man in the history of golf has had a greater influence and done as much to spread interest in the game to all parts of the globe.

Palmer won four U.S. Masters titles and for a long time Augusta was known as Palmersville. He won the U.S. Open in 1960 and has been second three times. He won the British Open at Royal Birkdale in 1961 and retained the title at Troon the following year. The one gap up to going to press is the U.S. P.G.A., and this is the one he regards as the ultimate achievement of his golfing life.

I first met him at the Canadian Open in 1967 and he told me that the secret of all golf under pressure was to remember to keep the swing slow and be sure to complete the backswing. I have tried to do this ever since. I played with him in Tokyo, Augusta, Jacksonville and more recently in a T.V. series. The more I see of him the more I admire him.

Those two words Arnold Palmer have a chemistry all their own. On both sides of the Atlantic he grabbed an ailing game by the scruff of the neck and through the thrilling aggression of his game and a magic appeal gave golf a new status. The British Open became great again because of his participation and prize money in the U.S. has soared from 100,000 dollars to seven million dollars since he began.

He is the embodiment of the all-American male with the build of a middleweight and the attacking power of a wing of jet fighters. At Carnoustie in 1968 he was bemoaning his poor form, and I said to him, 'I understand how you feel.' This most relaxed of men almost snapped back, 'You don't understand. You've never been where I've been, never been through what is happening to me now.' The all-time great who has such a burning desire to win had not been winning and he was angry at his decline. And with me for saying far too naïvely that I understood.

From his knock-kneed stance he could hole putts from any-
where and regularly did. His swing is more compact, more
repetitive than at any time in his career, but in spite of back-to-
back victories towards the end of 1969 we must take his word for
it that he no longer holes out like a winner.

The Americans use the word charisma to describe the appeal
of men like Palmer. He has been the most feted athlete of this
or any age and for years had an escort of half a dozen guards
to protect him from the fans wherever he played. Through it
all he remained courteous and completely unspoiled, aware of
his appeal, cashing in on it in a way no other sportsman has
ever done, but retaining a great humility.

The ranks of the biggest army ever to march in support of
one golfer have thinned a little but the forty-one-year-old
Arnold, winner of thirty major events between 1960 and 1963,
still commands a following of fans who would rather see him
shoot seventy-five than anyone else annihilate the course.

He loves flying and owns his own jet. At home his two
daughters serve wine and the label on the bottles is 'Chateau
Palmer'. His interests range through the whole spectrum of
modern life. He was the first in the field of commercial ex-
ploitation and counts his huge fortune in millions. His attractive
wife Winnie says of him, 'Arnold has everything a man could
want. It is no longer a question of money or glory or any of
those other things which mattered earlier on. If he feels he can
no longer win then I am sure he will quit. He is no longer
interested in being second and maybe only I know how much
he hates finishing in the pack.'

I have been told that I play the same adventurous golf. It is
a compliment which I value.

It never ceases to amaze me that when people talk of the great players one seldom hears the name of Casper. The golf world talked of the Big Three through the sixties and because he has never received the publicity which his golf warranted Casper has been something of a forgotten man.

There have been those who said that he is not the man for the big occasion. But he won the U.S. Open in 1959 and 1966 and in 1970 took the Masters. He appeared to have victory sewn up at Augusta the previous year but took forty to the turn in the last round and then a five at the tenth. He rated his golf in those first ten holes no better than that of a Sunday morning handi-capper and could not hide his disappoointment.

In spite of his failures in the U.S. P.G.A. and the British Open I rate him the finest all-round player in the world as golf moves into the seventies. He is a good driver and by suc-cessfully attacking the par five holes at Augusta in his victory year gave the lie to the suggestion that he cannot match the hitting of the giants. He is a marvellous wedge and sand wedge player and for a long time was considered the best putter in the world. He is probably still that. One could go to Nicklaus and say rightly that he is prone to missing short putts, to Palmer and suggest that he is a long way from being the best bunker player, but there are no such weaknesses in Casper's game.

A devout Mormon, he became known as Buffalo Bill because of a diet which included buffalo and reindeer steaks. It is probably years since he ate anything of the sort, but I did once see him ease his way through a dozen chops with masses of green vegetables at one sitting. He and his wife Shirley spend much of their time working for the church and he hands over a percentage of his winnings to the Mormons. They believe in sharing their riches and at the last count had five adopted children in addition to their own three.

Casper spends much of his time visiting U.S. forces abroad and has a disturbing habit of coming back from these trips and winning the first tournament in which he plays. I am like him in this respect in that I play better when I am fresh to golf.

Much is made of the fact that he does not believe in practice. There have been people like Hogan and Player who were born to work hard and who would never have been great had they not spent many hours each day hitting golf balls. Casper does not believe in this approach and an hour's session is as much as he allows himself unless there is a particular section of the game on which he feels he must work. His record proves that in his case this is the right preparation and it is ridiculous to suggest that he would have won more of the big events had he spent more time on his game.

That he is flexible in his views on particular golf courses was shown in the 1970 Masters. When Archer won in 1968 Billy treated the par fives as lay-up holes and in this way sacrificed shots on all of the four days which made the difference between winning and losing. By attacking them with all-out drives and big second shots he matched the big hitters and reaped the reward.

Like his good friend Gene Littler, whom he beat in the 1970 play-off, he treats the tour in a strictly business way and little is seen of him away from the course. He has never quite matched the commercial success of some other players and this worries those behind him. But I am not at all sure that it worries Casper, one of the nicest men in sport.

The reigning British Open champion Jack Nicklaus is in my view the greatest player in the world—when he wants to be. In six of the last seven years he has never been out of the first three in the money list and, bearing in mind the ever-growing competition and the fact that he takes long spells away from the tour, this was an incredible achievement.

British followers were surprised to see him looking so slim at St. Andrews. He had been dieting for a year (meat, chicken, green vegetables and five different sorts of citrus fruit a day) and at thirteen stones eight pounds was more than a stone lighter than on earlier visits to this country. It was taken by most of us in the field as a sign of just how badly Jack wanted to win at the home of golf.

A great amateur, he was still in the unpaid ranks when he finished second in the U.S. Open of 1960, and his aggregate score in the Opens of that year and 1959 was the lowest of the two fields. Jack turned professional in November 1961 and in the next six years won the Masters in 1963, 1965, 1966, the U.S. Open in 1962, the U.S. P.G.A. the following year and his first British Open in 1966. All of these great victories were achieved when under the greatest pressure from crowds who compared his so-called dullness, even surliness, with the outgoing gaiety and crowd appeal of the mighty Palmer. Of the comparison he said to me once, 'There was a certain strain. I was winning the big ones quite regularly but people sought reason to belittle me as a personality. I was not built the way Arnie was and could never match his appeal.

'But if I grimaced or looked unhappy about a shot or situation some press guys and a lot of people took it out of me. Had I tried a few gimmicks people would have accused me of apeing the big star. As it was I just kept on playing the best golf I could, sometimes resenting the criticism but generally having a ball.'

Nicklaus has a very real charm of his own and in recent years this has come through. At his home in Florida he keeps a card index of every course he has played, and when travelling to tournaments he briefs himself by studying these cards. He was, I believe, one of the first to make detail and feature notes of courses, a practice which has become standard today.

He is a terrific sportsman and although it may sound trite now that he has made his millions as a professional I really believe he still plays the game in a true amateur spirit. There are a lot of players on the U.S. tour who resent so-called 'foreigners' going over there and taking what they insist is 'their prize money' but Nicklaus takes the view that if you are good enough to beat them then you are entitled to walk away with the cash.

In its own way his golf is as bold as that of Palmer. I cannot believe that anyone has attacked the last four holes at Carnoustie as he did in the 1968 Open when fighting Player for the title and his drive over both necks of the burn at the seventeenth will be talked about whenever that particular championship is discussed.

Jack is held in especially high regard as an administrator and his home was the nerve centre of the so called 'rebel organisation' when it seemed likely that the tournament players would go it alone towards the end of the sixties. With Gardner Dickinson, Jack was in the forefront of a long and bitter battle which ended with the formation of the Tournament Players Division.

Anxious to campaign for the rights of the players, dedicated now to winning championships and tournaments of his choosing, he is, away from it all, a happy family man with three children who would as soon fish and shoot as play golf. In the late summer of 1969 he invited me on a fishing trip and, as I have always felt with him on the golf course, he seemed to be completely in charge. Watching him I sensed that here was someone with a Hemingway dedication to the pursuit of big fish and it was on that trip that he said of the impending Ryder Cup matches, 'Hey, Tony, here we are like couple of guys without a care in the world and in a few weeks time we will be at each other's throats . . . me for Uncle Sam, you for your jolly old queen and country.' As things worked out we played against each other once in the fourball foursomes and in both singles.

I enjoyed our matches on the last day at Royal Birkdale more than I suppose I had any right to do. My four and three win in the morning helped, of course, and our halved match in the afternoon was, perhaps, the most excitingly tough but friendly head-on clash I will ever have.

An incident at the long fifteenth proved what a marvellous sportsman Nicklaus is. I pulled my tee shot into a nasty lie near the boundary palings and as soon as we got to the ball Jack said I could have three free drops within two club lengths before playing the ball. When the ball landed in scrubby stuff he shouted, 'Pick it up from there, Tony. You don't have to play it until you have had two more drops.' I hacked out on to the fairway after the third drop and shall never forget his marvellous attitude at a critical stage of that last vital match of the series.

I remember too that familiar rueful grin and shake of the head when I holed a snaking putt from forty feet for an eagle three to halve the match at the seventeenth and the short chat we had after our drives at the eighteenth. I said I could never remember feeling as scared and he said with his arm on my shoulder, 'Don't worry, I feel the same way. Only maybe worse.' The whole match ended in a tie and it was Jack who did most of the lobbying afterwards which resulted in the U.S. officials suggesting that each country hold the Trophy for a year. It was, by rights, still American property as the tie entitled them to retain the pot presented by seed merchant Sam Ryder almost forty years earlier.

He is, of course, involved in business enterprises all over the world and on things he enjoys he spends money as if he had his own equivalent of our mint. One last aside from him, made when he talked to me for the first time of the size of his boat . . . 'It's pretty big. Sleeps six singles, twelve lovers!'

Gary Player burst onto the international golf scene in 1956 with a small frame, a flat highly suspect swing, a victory in Britain, and a desire as great as any man in the world to become a champion. Like Nicklaus he has achieved the Grand Slam and there is one competition which if it were played I would always back him to win.

We talk of world class performers but in golf there is no world championship as such. My idea would be to take the top twelve players and drop them down in the U.S., South Africa, Australia, Japan and Britain for a series of match play events with the winner decided on a league table basis. Golf is crying out for new ideas and I am sure sponsors could be found, with the final between the four men at the top being played in a different country each year.

I suggest Gary as the probable winner because he has won everywhere in all sorts of conditions, proving himself the most adaptable player of the modern era and more the complete international star than anyone. He has a wonderful record in the Open championships of South Africa and Australia and has won the British Open twice and the U.S. Open once. His success ratio in the U.S. since he first went there in 1958 is astonishingly high.

I particularly like him because to some extent I have faced similar problems and learned much from him. It is totally different for people like Gary and me to win in the U.S. because as we are playing in a foreign country the pressures are greater than on the home-bred players. He has taken on the Americans for a decade and more, commuting backwards and forwards from his home in Johannesburg, driving himself like mad for ten months or so of the year. Fortunately for him he is made of the same stuff as Hogan and thrives on the same unrelenting routine. He is very tough. I remember him telling me that in preparing for the Piccadilly World Match Play championship, which he has won three times, he had chopped down 500 trees on his farm back home. I suggested that he had done all this with a pen-knife and although he denied it I feel that he made a mental note that such an exercise might be an idea for some future build-up.

Being short he has always been forced to put every ounce of power into his long game. There are countless times when Nicklaus and Palmer can soft pedal a little on a drive but not Player. This has always meant that for Gary the slightest error in timing or swing position stood more chance of introducing errors . . . it is simply a case of being more likely to make mistakes when hitting every drive and long iron flat out. He has managed through superb fitness and strength and selfless dedication to build a swing able to stand up to the enormous strain of hitting at maximum power and only a man like Player could have done this. I have seen him completely drained after a day's duelling with bigger men and doubt if golf has been more exacting for anyone.

It was typical of him that after winning his second British Open he should say that he now looked forward to a second grand slam. But Nicklaus has greater reserves, and I would back him to complete a second four-timer before Player.

I have modelled my attitude to big golf more on Gary than on anyone else. The decision I took to play in the U.S. was partly motivated by his success there, and we have talked for hours on what is needed. He is a great believer in the philosophy that if the will is there everything is possible.

He has tried just about everything in his search for fitness, and although I have never gone to the extremes of yoga and health foods and a hundred or so press-ups on the fingertips before breakfast I am as aware as he is of the need for physical fitness and mental freshness. Against this background of dedication and sacrifice it seems so completely unjust that he should have been chosen as the target for anti-apartheid demonstrations.

The two glamour boys of the U.S. tour are undoubtedly Doug Sanders and Ray Floyd. Doug used to work non-stop on his playboy image and any references he made to the pedigree and habits of birds could not be checked in a volume on ornithology. He listed his hobbies as girls, drink, cigarettes and gambling and it is said that when he decided to live a little more quietly he gave up booze before ten in the morning.

Now he is married to an attractive former air hostess and they live in their fine Texas home. High up in the money list for many years he has yet to win a major championship and his disappointment at St. Andrews in losing the Open to Nicklaus was great.

He addresses the ball from a crab-like stance and gives it an almighty whack after the shortest backswing among the top players. In the Open he used a new mallet putter which he claimed gave him a better stroke and everyone was delighted to see this gay, amusing joker back near the top of the pack.

Floyd is a great character, wild and rampageous with a stream of good-looking girls around wherever he goes. With Doug married he has taken over as the most eligible beau on the tour and I have heard some people say that his exploits make those of Sanders look like those of a baptist minister on a health cure.

His outlook on golf is refreshing. He says that he only practises when shamed into doing so by other people. He hits the ball huge distances and won three tournaments in 1969. Like Sanders in the old days he considers any time before mid-day as strictly for himself and a pretty companion but in spite of the lean time he had after the great successes of 1969 I suggest that he will be one of the big stars of the seventies.

Lee Trevino has won a great reputation as a clown and this has often led to him being underrated as a player. He broke through after years as one of the tour's journeymen with victory in the U.S. Open at Rochester in 1968 and has replied to those who considered that win a flash in the pan with a string of subsequent successes.

Lee hits the ball low and very straight and for this reason is at his best on flat courses. People like him are great for golf, for the game is an entertainment and he has the great gift of involving the crowd in the action. He is exactly what he appears to be, a happy dumpy extrovert who wants everyone to join in his fun. Had Lee not existed someone would have had to invent him. But behind the fooling and non-stop banter there is a truly great golfer.

Orville Moody followed Trevino as a shock winner of the U.S. Open but although he is a very talented player I do not believe he has got the desire or the flair of Trevino. He was a good player for years while in the U.S. Army but seems unlikely to follow up his Open victory with the sort of success Trevino has had. But he will certainly make a lot more than he did as an army sergeant.

Tony Lema's death in an air crash was a great loss to the game for after years of struggle he had hit the top and was being talked of as the new member of what had become the big four. On his first trip to Britain he won the Open by five shots from Nicklaus and many considered his golf at St. Andrews in 1964 to be as near to perfection as had ever been seen in the championship.

Like Palmer, 'Champagne Tony' had a magic all his own. There was something feline about his walk and everything about his game was classical. He had won three tournaments in a row before coming over for the Open and those who thought that he was taking a liberty with the Old Course by arriving only a couple of days before serious action began were soon eating their words.

Lema, a one-time stevedore in the docks at San Francisco, had the most classical swing among modern golfers and had he lived would certainly have become one of the all time greats. Like Snead he never appeared to hit the ball hard but he was in fact one of the most powerful men in golf.

Tom Weiskopf is one of my best chums on the U.S. tour and he came over to Lincolnshire to spend Christmas with Viv and me. I am probably prejudiced, but having watched all the great players all over the world I believe he is potentially one of the best.

Like Nicklaus, he finds it easy to flight the ball high with the long irons, clear the traps and stop it on the greens. He has not got a bad shot but has lost many tournaments he should have won because his temperament got the better of him.

This has hampered him a lot. I do not think his temper is any worse than that of many players but he is a perfectionist and gets really mad when what he feels has been the perfect shot does not have the perfect end. He works terribly hard on staying calm and his beautiful wife Jeannie has been a great help, for they both know that his golf has not produced the results it merits.

He hits through the year more good shots per round than anyone else. Sometimes his long iron play is unbelievable, three or four times in a round he will hit three irons to within a couple of feet of the flag. To play this sort of super accurate golf and not score well all the time must be murder, but I am sure he will be one of the dominating players of the next decade.

Bert Yancey, a former West Point cadet, is with Weiskopf my closest buddy on the tour and I have learned a lot about the golf swing from him. He is a great theorist and lectures at P.G.A. schools and universities on the mechanics of the swing.

This great knowledge of what really happens during the stroke sometimes affects his game. He is always experimenting and working on new ideas, and gets bogged down by theory. On a practice day before the Crosby I remember him saying,

'Tony, what do you think of this?' I said, 'For God's sake Bert just go out there and play. It breaks my heart to see someone as good as you keep screwing up his game.' He won the tournament so maybe what I said went home.

He had a great year in 1967 when he won three times, and twice he has been third in the Masters. We all get depressed at times and when he had that eighty in the Open at Carnoustie he was in a really bad state. Like Weiskopf he has yet to win as often as he should but both have this wonderful game and will support it with results one day.

Frank Beard is a phlegmatic sort of chap who plays golf like he has a computer instead of a brain. He is a stonewaller, having worked it out through the years that the only risks you can afford to take are calculated ones. Basically Frank is content to play for pars, giving himself the chance to make the occasional birdie but concentrating generally on avoiding bogeys.

This defensive attitude does not make for exciting golf but Frank insists that he is only in the game to provide for his family. He has an office worker mentality and says that he does not give a can of beans about winning. He is always sneaking into third or fourth place relying on the others making the mistakes, and he invariably finishes high in the money list after appearing to have done little all season. But in 1969 he really started to win, and ended up top of the list, winning twice, finishing in the top three eight times and earning around 185,000 dollars in prize money. This is the performance of a great player.

Peter Thomson dominated the game in Britain for a number of years, winning five Open championships and domestic tournaments with a regularity which must have embarrassed the home professionals. Golf has fewer more charming, more intelligent men and he has revolutionised the game in his own country and the Far East.

He has a reputation for being impatient with the press and has, I believe, been difficult to interview. Peter is very much a loner and would rather lock himself away with his books and classical music than join the boys at the bar.

A persistent critic of the game in the U.S., he has always preferred to campaign on courses and in countries in which he feels all round shot making is required as opposed to power, and where he can show himself to be the great artist he is.

Second to the great South African Bobby Locke at Royal Lytham and St. Annes in 1952, joint second again the following year behind Hogan at Carnoustie, Thommo, as he is known with a mixture of affection and apprehension ('How's Thommo doing?' one hears people say whenever he is in the field) won with a total of 283 at Royal Birkdale in 1954. He completed a hat-trick of victories at St. Andrews (281) and Hoylake (286). Then in 1958 he beat Thomas in a play-off at Royal Lytham, and in 1965 he got to within one of Vardon's record number of triumphs with a total of 285, again at Royal Birkdale.

Peter really set his stall out that year. Only after he had won did he reveal that three months earlier he had sneaked into Britain and made a five-day reconnaissance of the Lancashire course with his heavyweight caddie Jackie Leonard.

Says Peter, 'I hate tricked-up courses, weird pin placings like they have at the Masters. Golf began on the natural terrain of places like St. Andrews and the records show that the best players win there. It is because the championship courses in

Britain demand an all-round mastery of shot making that I prefer them. Golf is not just a slammer's game.'

We differ completely on this point, but paradoxically I have a great regard for Thomson's views.

Roberto de Vicenzo, whose popularity in South America stands second only to the soccer wonderman Pele, finally won the Open championship on which he had set his heart throughout a long career at Hoylake in 1967. He first challenged for it at Muirfield in 1948, finishing joint third behind Henry Cotton, was second to Locke at Sandwich and Troon, seventh behind Hogan at Carnoustie, third to Thomson in 1956, fifth to Nagle in the centenary Open, third to Lema in 1964, and fourth to Thomson in 1965.

I do not have to mention that my eyes were very much on him on the last day at Royal Lytham. As we changed for the final round he looked up from tying his shoelaces and said with a huge grin, 'You win today, Tony. Roberto too old now, no putt good. You get a good start and no one catch you.'

Strangely, his popularity was never higher than in defeat. I am referring, of course, to the U.S. Masters the year after his Hoylake victory when his partner Tommy Aaron wrongly marked his card. Roberto signed for a four instead of a three and although actually level with Bob Goalby was placed second. 'What a stupid I am!' said the best long iron player I have ever seen . . . and rushed off to congratulate the 'winner'.

Henry Cotton won three Opens and gave the professional golfer a new standing in Britain. I was unfortunate enough never to see him in his prime, but having played with him at his course in Penina can assure the millions who hold the old maestro in such high esteem that he is still playing well. He often has a rather unusual caddie, a donkey called Pacifico who carries his bags and at times gives him a lift.

In 1965 he awarded me his 'Rookie of the Year' prize of £100. Shy and nervous at a rather high-powered gathering in his Eaton-Square flat, I helped myself to a couple of cigarettes and had three lagers. The following Sunday he wrote in his column that 'young professionals who want to do really well should not drink or smoke'. I often wonder how direct a reference this was.

X

Reflections

X

Reflections

The rewards after a comparatively short time at the top can be startling and later in this chapter I will give a description of the kind of marketing operations negotiated on my behalf. I feel in no way a pawn in some huge international finance game; and I am aware enough of the position I hold and hope to hold in golf not to allow these outside activities to interfere with my game.

Palmer became sport's most saleable figure after winning the first of his four U.S. Masters titles in 1958. We once went through his diary for the following month and with something short of enthusiasm he pointed out that in thirty days he was due to play tournaments, give exhibitions, make appearances at and attend business meetings in five different countries. Yet in spite of the incredible pressures—far greater than I will ever know—he stayed at the top for at least a decade and today, at forty-one, remains one of the game's biggest attractions.

I had experience of an overcrowded schedule before the British Open of 1970. Plans to film the T.V. series with Palmer and other matches had been made months earlier but what had not been foreseen was the extra work brought about by my

U.S. Open victory. The schedule of that crowded fifteen days will not, I hope, ever have to be repeated.

With the fruits of two major victories in the space of forty-nine weeks came the inevitable criticism and a certain amount of sniping. I read in a British golf magazine that I had a reputation for meanness. Maybe I ought to have sent the writer, whom I hardly know, a bottle of champagne to celebrate Chaska, but one cannot help but be a little distressed by such comments, particularly when the writer neither knows me well, nor understands the actual pressures of professional golf.

I value money as much as anyone who has worked hard to get it, and have no intention of being careless with it; but I like to spend fairly freely on myself and my family and at the moment have a great wish to own a Rolls-Royce. This is not, as might be suggested, indicative of a change in the size of my hat. I am a car fanatic. Since my first A30 I have had eleven different ones, and have always cherished the idea of driving the best car in the world.

I have been told that at times I speak with an American accent. There are some words here and there on which I sometimes go a little transatlantic, but I have lived for the major part of the last four years with Americans and find myself naturally talking that way.

The mail is full of surprises. I did some advertising for Black and White whisky. Those who felt concerned about this can rest assured that although I enjoy the odd glass of scotch I am in no danger of becoming addicted. But as a result of this advertisement I received a strange letter from a solicitor warning me that the time on the watch I was wearing showed ten past three and that I had therefore been guilty of drinking outside licensing hours!

Life has, as you will appreciate, changed considerably, for I am told that I can now earn as much for an exhibition game and clinic as I did on the British circuit in 1967 when my prize money was £3,393. But my attitude to people has not changed although even my closest friends tend to treat me as a different person to the one they knew. It is a hard feeling to explain, and one that will hopefully disappear. I have more possessions (I've got a thing about collecting watches and shoes), lead a full and allegedly glamorous life, and at twenty-six can do almost anything I wish. But I am the same sort of bloke who likes to swap stories with his mates, and to enjoy a friendly game of golf. Most of all I like to entertain at home, perhaps because it is such a comparatively new experience. Scunthorpe, or the part of it where I grew up, is a marvellous place but not exactly famed for its dinner parties, and we find people are themselves in the informality of our new house.

When I got back from the U.S. Open I bady needed a haircut. In the first couple of days I found out what it meant to be a celebrity in a small town and got no peace at all. All I wanted was a nice quiet haircut by the barber who had been doing my hair for years, but I had to ring him and ask if I could go down to his shop at six-thirty when all the other customers had gone. There is, understandably, a great interest at home in a local lad who has become internationally famous, and at week-ends people drive to Elsham just to see us and our new home.

It is generally accepted that golf is sixty per cent psychological. When playing in tournaments I like to get a routine going so that nothing out of the way crops up to disturb my concentration. I make sure I know how long it takes to get to the golf course so that I have plenty of time to change and warm up for my usual thirty minutes or so on the practice ground. And I always take plenty of clothes with me, for it is a professional's duty, as an entertainer, to look smartly, if not flamboyantly, dressed. Discipline means a lot, and a great deal of nervous and physical energy can be wasted on seemingly trivial things.

One of the most carefully planned preparations was by Gary Player before his 1965 U.S. Open victory at Bellerive, St. Louis. Gary wrote afterwards that as far as the Big Three were concerned he felt the odd man out, both as a foreigner and, because of his size. Success at Bellerive would make him the first of the illustrious trio to achieve the Grand Slam.

Gary went to the course ten days before the championship and made extensive notes on the lay-out. He wrote down a list of do's and don'ts concerning his personal approach and admitted that he almost accepted the offer of a hypnotist who called regularly at his hotel to work on his mental attitude. He decided that as he had tended for some time to get excited during tournaments he would do everything slowly ... drive his car slowly, shave and bathe slowly, everything in slow motion. He had also been inclined to chat to the galleries between shots and this habit must also be curbed. He added of that prelude to the final act of achieving the Grand Slam, 'I got the message. It is an indescribable feeling, which I have had four or five times in my life, the positive, powerful feeling, indeed certainty, that I was going to win the championship.'

Do golfers get such feelings? It has never happened to me, but I must admit that there have been times when the possibility of victory seemed stronger than on other occasions. It is a feeling that everything is going to go right, the knowledge that the putter is hot and friendly; and when I get this the confidence flows back through the rest of my game. It is not a question of lifting my game to a peak for the big occasion but of recognising that with normal luck my mental shape and the state of my game is good enough to win. After that there is the little matter of proving these things over four days and seventy-two holes.

The strain of big golf is often underrated. A golf tournament lasts a heck of a long time. With fighters or footballers the action is over a sprint period. The tension builds up all the time in golf ... one plays the shot, wonders during the walk to the next blow just how one will make it, clings to a favourable situation created by a few birdies, and sleeps on the triumphs of one day and the challenge of the next. Little wonder that I sometimes have to take a pill, and enforce sleep.

I am not saying that I would rather be a footballer or boxer. I am earning a good living playing the game I love. But the tensions are there and we are all aware of them. As a kid I used to practise believing that Hogan or Snead was looking over my shoulder. I tried then to put myself under pressure, and avoid hitting unnecessarily 'loose' shots and to learn to hit good shots even when physically tired. Even now, on the practice ground, I sometimes imagine myself in a pressure situation.

I know when my game is right because after a few shots I can see the shape of the trajectory of the ball before I hit it. I see the fairway lay-out, the bunkers guarding the green, and can visualise in sharp focus exactly which path the ball should take. This thing happens when I am relaxed, completing my backswing and swinging slow. And using the legs properly.

The decision to go with Mark McCormack which I took in

1967 was without doubt the most important of my career. If that sounds like an endorsement for McCormack I make no apology. Palmer, Nicklaus and Player all suggested to me during my early trips to the U.S. and on their visits to Britain that I might one day join him, and as a result I have been able to concentrate on golf while other people look after travel, hotel bookings and the considerable business activities in which I am now involved.

The organisation which began when Mark, a Cleveland lawyer, took over Palmer's affairs in 1959 is now world wide. There are offices in more than a dozen major cities and the staff, handpicked and young, now numbers more than a hundred. Ed Keating looks after my affairs in America and in Britain Malcolm Hamer recently joined the staff to make sure that things go smoothly for me. Mark visits Britain several times a year and he has a payroll of twelve in his Park Street, London, office where Sarah Chappell, his very charming first recruit, remains a great friend to us all.

The McCormack net has widened considerably since he first set Palmer and Co. on the millionaire path and his clients now include Jean Shrimpton and other top models, Jackie Stewart, bridge player, Jeremy Flint, and song writer Barry Mason, who is doing a song which I am going to record during the winter. As a bath-room star, I can say no more as yet than that I like what I have heard of the song.

Stewart is a wonderful character and we have often talked informally about the widely contrasting pressures associated with our two sports. At the end of these discussions I find myself full of admiration for champions like him, realising that of all sports, motor-racing demands most from its stars.

The busines ventures under the supervision of an accountant in the London office, Martin Sorrell, got under way shortly after the British Open in 1969, and I am 'now associated with an amazing range of concerns and companies': Pan American; Sea Island, Georgia; Ajay Enterprises, U.S.A.; Dunlop Sports Co.; Colgate-Palmolive; Bata Shoes; Meridian Clothing Co.; Richards and Thirkwell Headwear; Wolsey Socks; Taunton and Thorne Golf Gloves; Black and White Whisky; Faywick Flexi Grips; National Cash Register Co.; *Daily Express* (features and instructional strip); *Golf World*; and the *Sunday Express*; not to mention the publishers of this book both here and in U.S.A.

Coping with the demands of these organisations means that I must spend a lot of time away from the golf course, and my golf stretches far beyond the tournament circuit, as I play in more and more television challenge matches.

My own company, Tony Jacklin Enterprises, has been formed and will have its headquarters in London. In addition to all of these things there are dinners to attend ... I worked out after the British Open that I could have eaten out every night for three months and still not have satisfied all of the people who so kindly wanted me to be their guest.

Golf is booming in Britain but compared with America and Japan we are not keeping pace with the demand for courses. The Americans now build 'instant' courses in less than six months and between 1957 and 1966 the number of courses rose from 57 to 360 in Japan. The trend there is to build 'freeway lay-outs', courses with very few bunkers and no rough so that the maximum number of people can get round in a day. It is not necessary to stud courses with large numbers of bunkers and although water hazards are desirable they are costly to construct and not conducive to fast play.

There have been a few moments of crisis between the P.G.A.'s of Britain and America and I am sure an annual meeting between the heads of the two associations would benefit the professional game in both countries. We in Britain must face the fact that we are very much the minnow in the prize money pool but it should be possible to ensure that some of the big names from the U.S. tour play in our bigger events, if there is more careful long term planning. Even now, there are slots on the U.S. tour and new sponsors should work on the basis that they have a far better chance of success if they launch their tournament to coincide with these free weeks.

The Americans are heading towards a second 'satellite' tour. There are now ten events on this mini-tour and players will graduate from these to the big one where the prize money may soon reach the staggering sum of 10,000,000 dollars. Mr. Joe Dey, boss of the U.S. Tournament Players Division, expects to have two complete tours in operation by the mid-seventies.

The influences on my career have been many and varied and I am appreciative of all the help which has so freely come my way. I might never have swopped soccer for golf had my Dad not taken up the game, and when I did so both he and my Mother were always on hand to give me the encouragement I needed. I was always a stubborn little devil and by doing things like paper rounds and my Saturday morning stint in Scunthorpe market I was able to pay for equipment and clothes. But we are a very close family and I am happy these days to be able to share my many new experiences with them. All I would like is to persuade grandfather David Jacklin to cross the Atlantic one day, but, at eighty he says he would not be happy leaving his motor bike and gardening jobs.

My sister Lynn and her husband spent three weeks at Sea Island after the 1970 Masters and their son Darran is already swinging a useful cut down five iron. Old chums like Jack Powell and Alan Williamson come to the house a lot when we are at home and I still enjoy taking a few bob off them on the course.

At Potters Bar, Mrs. Baker always looked after me like a son and worked miracles with my laundry so that I always had clean clothes to wear from my very limited wardrobe. Bill Shankland appeared tough on me in those days but the long hours on the practice ground and the 'disciplinary' spells selling in the shop were of much greater value than I thought them to be at the time.

Jack Rubin and Wally Dubabny gave me financial help when I needed it and still pop up in various parts of Britain and the world, and I must thank them for the two memorable dinners they gave for me after winning at Jacksonville and Royal Lytham. Then there are men like Eric Hayes, George Carr and Tony Carter of Dunlop who gave me the much-needed financial help in the early days when a couple of hundred pounds meant the difference between gaining experience in the sun of South Africa and staying at home in the wind and rain of an English winter. At Sea Island more recently Irv Harden, Eddie Thomson and Hugh Johnson have been real pals.

As a new boy I could not have been received more warmly by most of the players, particularly by Palmer, Nicklaus, Player, Yancey and Weiskopf. I learned much from all of them . . . so much about the golf game, about America and the vital business of living through the pressures of the tournament scene, and about life itself.

Finally, Vivien. Neither of us had done much in life to speak of when we met and I have been lucky in having someone like her with whom to share all that has happened to me since we met. There have been times of deep depression and I doubt if I could have ridden them had she not been with me. She has tramped round the courses of the world, watching from the wings, catching my eye among the huge crowds when the one thing I wanted more than anything was to look into the face of the girl I love.

We are both terribly proud of Bradley, the little smiler who took my mind off things for a while before the last round at Chaska and who at eight months can take my mind off almost anything I am doing which is why so far he has not seen much of his old man playing golf.

Thanks to everyone in Britain, and America who have made this short journey so memorable. But most especially, to Vivien.

Appendix

Appendix

Tony Jacklin

Career Record 1963–69

Schedule of tournament winnings

T = tied
In Match Play events, finish recorded by round when defeated

1963 : British circuit—

Tournament	Finish	Score	Prizemoney £		
Cox Moore	34	290	9	10	0
Gor-Ray	14	296	20	8	6
Open Championship	30	295	56	13	4
News of the World	2nd round		38	0	0
Senior Service	Tied 25	284	161	10	0
Combe Hill Assistants	T 2	218	45	0	0

Total P.G.A.-listed winnings, including minor events, for the year: £408 11s. 10d.

1964: British circuit—

Tournament	Finish	Score	Prizemoney £
Schweppes	11	294	148 8 9
Swallow Penfold	26	306	79 19 2
Coombe Hill Assistants	1	285	100 0 0
Daks	T 18	295	53 4 0
Bowmaker	T 45	152	10 0 0
Carrolls Sweet Afton	27	282	57 10 0
Pringle	T 31	315	71 5 0
News of the World	1st round		23 15 0
Braemar	T 17	299	85 10 0
Piccadilly	T 34	141	68 1 8
Rediffusion	T 18	278	66 10 0

Total P.G.A. winnings for the year: £764 3s. 6d.

1965: British circuit—

Tournament	Score	Finish	Prizemoney £
Schweppes	8	293	178 15 0
Swallow Penfold	T 31	299	73 2 6
Martini	38	294	25 0 0
Jeyes	T 22	290	36 11 3
Silent Night	T 31	301	70 13 9
Pringle	T 5	284	238 17 6
Bowmaker	T 38	145	10 15 3
Open Championship	T 25	298	66 5 0
Carrolls	15	282	100 0 0
Senior Service	T 12	211	133 5 0
Gor-Ray	1	283	290 0 0
News of the World	Semi-finals		243 15 0
Dunlop Masters	T 15	294	41 8 9
Rediffusion	T 25	284	30 17 6
Piccadilly	3	273	341 5 0
Smart Weston	T 6	144	61 13 4
Cutty Sark Southern	1	138	200 0 0
Gallagher Ulster Open	T 13	281	36 5 0

Total P.G.A. winnings for the year: £1,780 11s. 6d.

1965: American P.G.A. circuit—

Tournament	Finish	Score	U.S. Dollars
Carling World Open	T 34	290	1,005.00

1966: British circuit—

Tournament	Finish	Score	Prizemoney £		
Schweppes	T 5	289	179	8	0
Penfold Swallow	T 3	283	302	5	0
Agfa-Gevaert	T 3	279	199	17	6
Martini	3	279	500	0	0
Daks	T 7	289	97	10	0
Jeyes	T 23	219	39	0	0
Pringle	T 16	284	48	15	0
Bowmaker	T 45	154	10	15	3
Open Championship	T 30	298	102	0	0
Esso Round Robin	11	11 points	220	0	0
Carrolls	3	277	383	6	8
News of the World	4th round		97	10	0
Dunlop Masters	T 23	296	43	17	6
Rediffusion	2	268	341	5	0

Total P.G.A. winnings for the year: £2,715 9s. 11d.

1966: South African tour—

Tournament	Finish	Score	Prizemoney Rand
P.G.A. Championship	T 23	298	Nil
Western Province Open	T 6	295	118.33
General Motors Open	T 7	295	182.50
Transvaal Open	T 6	284	275
Natal Open	T 5	295	166.66
Dunlop Masters	T 3	282	375
South African Open	9	286	90
Kimberley	T 1	273	600

1966: New Zealand tour—

Tournament	Finish	Score	Prizemoney N.Z. £
New Zealand Open	5	291	125
Watties	2	271	225
Wills Masters	T 23	301	Nil
B.P.	5	283	150
Metalcraft	T 13	289	30
N.Z. Forest Products	T 1	272	350
Caltex	T 13	294	50

1966: Partnered Peter Alliss to give England tenth place in the Canada Cup International played at the Yomiuri Country Club, Tokyo, Japan. Jacklin finished joint sixteenth in the individual competition with 284 total.

1967: British circuit—

Tournament	Finish	Score	Prizemoney £		
Schweppes	42	296	19	10	0
Penfold	T 20	282	40	4	4
Agfa-Gevaert	T 33	291	23	3	2
Daks	24	294	39	0	0
P.G.A. Close Championship	T 6	282	103	0	0
Martini	T 10	285	145	0	0
Pringle	1	283	731	5	0
Open Championship	5	285	775	0	0
Esso Round Robin	T 8	13 points	260	0	0
News of the World	2nd round		39	0	0
Dunlop Masters	1	274	1,218	15	0

Total P.G.A. winnings for the year: £3,393 17s. 6d.

1967: American P.G.A. circuit—

Tournament	Finish	Score	Prizemoney U.S. Dollars
Masters	T 16	292	2,100
Canadian Open	T 12	284	3,773.87
American Golf Classic	T 59	295	Nil
Carling World Open	T 7	285	4,325.00
Hawaiian Open	T 11	289	2,125.00
Caracas Open	8	280	700.00
Peurto Rico Open	T 45	308	Nil
West End Classic	T 14	288	375.00

American P.G.A. winnings for the year: 12,323 dollars and 87 cents for eighty-third place on the official money list.

1967: Far East tour—

Tournament	Finish	Score	Prizemoney Dollars
Singapore Open	T 40	299	24.44
Malaysian Open	T 5	288	597.21
Thailand Open	T 2	287	1,033.33
Hong Kong Open	T 15	280	196

1967: Australia tour—

Tournament	Finish	Score	Prizemoney Aust. Dollars
Victoria Open	T 3	287	437

1967: New Zealand tour—

Tournament	Finish	Score	Prizemoney N.Z. Dollars
Stars Travel Tournament	1 (after play-off)	274	600

1967: Ryder Cup match—

Foursomes: Jacklin and Dave Thomas defeated Doug Sanders and Gay Brewer four and three, and Gene Littler and Al Geiberger by three and two.

Fourball: Jacklin and Thomas lost to Littler and Geiberger by one hole and halved with Littler and Geiberger.

Singles: Jacklin lost to Arnold Palmer three and two and lost to Gardner Dickinson three and two.

1968: British circuit—

Tournament	Finish	Score	Prizemoney £		
Open Championship	T 18	299	255	0	0
Dunlop Masters	T 8	282	182	16	3
P.G.A. Close Championship	3	278	375	7	6
Piccadilly World Match-Play	semi-final		1,095	0	0

Total P.G.A. winnings for the year: £2,763 3s. 9d.

1968 : American P.G.A. circuit —

Tournament	Finish	Score	Prizemoney U.S. Dollars
Bing Crosby	T 10	291	1,840.00
Kaiser	T 44	288	312.50
Bob Hope	T 60	364	Nil
Tucson Open	T 8	278	2,950
Doral Open	T 43	291	320.00
Florida Citrus Open	T 4	277	5,347.50
Pensacola Open	T 2	269	7,800.00
Jacksonville Open	1	273	20,000.00
Masters	T 22	288	1,760.00
Tournament of Champions	T 7	283	5,750.00
Byron Nelson Classic	T 17	282	1,450.00
Houston Champions	T 47	291	225.00
Greater New Orleans Open	T 42	286	292.86
Colonial National	T 19	290	1,550.00
Atlanta Classic	T 54	296	Nil
'500' Festival Open	T 42	291	320.00
Cleveland Open	T 6	280	3,776.67
Western Open	T 56	292	Nil
American Golf Classic	T 40	289	498.75
Westchester Classic	T 23	282	2,034.72

Total American P.G.A. winnings for the year: 58,495 dollars and 17 cents for twenty-ninth place on the official money list.

1968 : Australia tour—

Tournament	Finish	Score	Prizemoney Aust. Dollars
Wills Masters	T 17	290	136.67
Dunlop International	T 3	287	1,250

1969 : British circuit—

Tournament	Finish	Score	Prizemoney £
Open Championship	1	280	4,250 0 0
Piccadilly Medal	3rd round		121 17 6
Dunlop Masters	T 3	285	487 10 0
Piccadilly World Match-Play	1st round		1,121 5 0

Total P.G.A. winnings for the year : £5,980 12s. 6d.

1969: American P.G.A. circuit—

Tournament	Finish	Score	Prizemoney U.S. Dollars
Los Angles Open	T 34	286	530.00
Kaiser	T 14	140	885.00
Bing Crosby	T 31	292	739.83
Andy Williams	T 15	290	2,250.00
Bob Hope	T 13	353	1,800.00
Pheonix	T 60	279	142.86
Doral	T 8	282	4,237.50
Florida Open	T 72	293	143.75
Jacksonville	T 37	288	460.00
National Airlines	T 12	283	3,428.57
U.S. Masters	Failed to qualify for final 36 holes		1,000
Colonial	T 53	293	200
Western Open	T 5	284	4,302.00
U.S. Open Championship	T 25	289	1,300
Kemper Open	T 5	280	5,193.75
Cleveland Open	T 61	290	191.30
Canadian Open	T 39	292	406.10
P.G.A. Championship	T 25	287	1,300
Sahara	T 5	278	3,850.00

Total American P.G.A. winnings for the year: 33,036 dollars for sixtieth place on the official money list.

1969: Australia tour—

Tournament	Finish	Score	Prizemoney Aust. Dollars
Australian Open	T 35	305	90
Dunlop International	4	280	1,900

1969: Ryder Cup match—

Foursomes: Jacklin and Peter Townsend defeated Dave Hill and Tommy Aaron three and one, and Billy Casper and Frank Beard two up.

Fourball: Jacklin and Neil Coles defeated Jack Nicklaus and Dan Sikes one up and halved with Lee Trevino and Miller Barber.

Singles: Jacklin defeated Nicklaus four and three and halved with Nicklaus.